Doing the Right Things
for the Right Reasons

by Richard L. Bednar
and
Scott R. Peterson

Deseret Book Company
Salt Lake City, Utah

*To my mother, Lois Avery Peterson, who does
the right things for the right reasons*

Library of Congress Cataloging-in-Publication Data

Bednar, Richard L.
   Doing the right things for the right reasons / by Richard L.
Bednar and Scott R. Peterson.
      p.   cm.
   Includes bibliographical references and index.
   ISBN 0-87579-870-5 (hardbound)
   1. Spiritual life—Mormon Church. 2. Self-realization—
Religious aspects—Mormon Church. 3. Self-esteem—Religious
aspects—Mormon Church. 4. Mormon Church—Doctrines.
I. Peterson, Scott R. II. Title
BX8656.B439   1995
241'.049332—dc20   95-12512
                                                        CIP

Printed in the United States of America

10 9   8   7   6   5   4   3   2   1

....

CONTENTS

....

PREFACE

In many ways, this book is a continuation of our previous one, *Spirituality and Self-Esteem: Developing the Inner Self.* In that book we looked at the relationship between psychological well-being and spiritual strength and talked about the need to cope with adversity and opposition as a way to improve the inner self. In this book we develop that theme further and introduce a concept that offers a way to cultivate the ability to do the right things for the right reasons, particularly in moments of difficulty and opposition.

CHAPTER ONE

RIGHTEOUS SELF-GOVERNMENT

YOU ARE ALONE. YOU CAN DO ANYTHING YOU WANT. No family, no church, no authority figure will monitor or judge you. No one will stop you no matter what you do. No one will ever know. No one will even care. You are completely on your own. What kind of person are you? Kind and thoughtful? Demanding and selfish? Fearful and inhibited? Pleasure seeking and corrupt? If your behavior were a natural extension of who you are deep down inside, would you behave in the same way you do now? How different is this real, unfettered you from the one you typically let those around you see?

What we are and what we appear to be represent our "private" and our "public" selves. Each of us has both. The public self is socially appropriate. It gauges how we think we are perceived by others and adjusts itself accordingly. It can cover pain, hide fear, mask disagreement, and represent us in ways that may not truly reflect what we think or feel. It can be proper and impressive, yet fickle and fake.

The private self, on the other hand, is our essential self. It is our true character. It is the fountain of our intent, whether good or bad. It is how we would be understood if others could open us up like a book and read without the distraction of a pleasing cover designed to enhance sales—just a truthful,

1

straightforward text defining the quality of our motives, the nature of our heart, and the intent of our soul.

It is incredibly important to accurately discern our own motives, largely because society emphasizes positive impressions and appearances regardless of whether they are real. In the words of a recent television ad, "Image is everything." Looking good seems more important than being good. And looking good is all too often just another way of saying we've gained the attention and approval of others.

Whether we are at home, on the job, or in church, why we do what we do tells us more about the person we really are than does our behavior alone. Anyone can look good. We can do favors for each other, agree with one another, and do what we are asked to do, and if appearances counted for everything, we would be heaven-bound. But what if our motives could be as easily discerned as our actions? What would we see then? Would tranquility at home be merely silence spawned from fear of being hurt or rejected? Would agreeing with the boss be simply a way to avoid conflict? Would home teaching or visiting teaching be done out of grudging obligation rather than a true love and concern for one another?

The epitome of spiritual strength and psychological health is the point at which our actions are godlike because our motives are godlike. Or, as Nephi said, "Follow the Son, with full purpose of heart, acting no hypocrisy and no deception before God, but with real intent, repenting of your sins, witnessing unto the Father that ye are willing to take upon you the name of Christ" (2 Nephi 31:13).

Behaving with such sincerity is no small task. It requires moving away from managing outward appearances to cultivating inward substance. It means keeping our integrity intact by refraining from avoiding conflict, by expressing tender feelings that may leave us feeling vulnerable. It may mean, for example, telling our priesthood or Relief Society leader that we won't participate in a service project because we don't feel charitable, instead of saying we're busy, and then, even more important, acknowledging to the Lord our lack of charity and asking for forgiveness and help in overcoming that fault. It may mean likening ourselves to the Nephites called by King Benjamin to repent and experience a "mighty change" of heart—a call that would be echoed in these latter days, nearly two millennia later, by other living prophets (Mosiah 5:2).

Such profound change usually comes only after deeply questioning ourselves and then eliminating what stops us from reaching our mortal and eternal potential. We simply must understand the truth about ourselves now before we can hope to become something better later. Acknowledging the truth about ourselves means we must become aware of both our weaknesses and our strengths. When performed honestly, such personal scrutiny can produce great discontent, but it is exactly that discontent that fuels our desire to change.

Regrettably, however, many of us are far too eager to hide our weaknesses. We fail to understand that the problem is not that we have weaknesses but that we refuse to acknowledge them. The truth is, unless we acknowledge them, we cannot overcome them. Instead, we try to avoid the pain of recognizing our weaknesses by hiding them. We run the risk of being, in the words of President Spencer W. Kimball, "a people who are pure in appearance, rather [than] a people who are pure in heart" (*The Teachings of Spencer W. Kimball,* ed. Edward L. Kimball [Salt Lake City: Bookcraft Inc., 1982], 363).

A term that describes purity of both motive and behavior, a

term that captures the sum and substance of doing the right things for the right reasons, is *righteous self-government*. It is the moral exercise of agency in the face of psychological conflict and potential spiritual compromise. It is the ability to face personal weaknesses with humility and resolve to make them strengths. It is spiritual and psychological character in action. In this sense, the "mighty change" must come from the inside out, so that our outward behavior becomes a natural expression of our righteous inward desires. Mere conformity to commandments, obligations, and duties is not enough. Righteous self-government requires authentic love for Christ and personal integrity that naturally produce sincere Christian works.

Such authenticity also enables us to confront opposition without avoidance and self-deception. Those who close their eyes to their weaknesses remain weak. And to the weak, running from conflict and opposition only reinforces their weakness. But the Lord has promised those who choose to face their failings, "Because thou hast seen thy weakness thou shalt be made strong" (Ether 12:37).

Interestingly, a large body of evidence from the behavioral sciences arrives at the same conclusion: individual agency and a deeply ingrained willingness to face problems are essential ingredients of emotional well-being. Many prominent researchers have demonstrated that although everyone unavoidably experiences psychological stress, the best way to weather emotional difficulties is to face them rather than to deny that they exist.

The connection between spiritual development and psychological health is one reason that righteous self-government can play a crucial role in our mortal happiness. By doing the right things for the right reasons, particularly when we would just as soon avoid the discomfort those actions might bring, we become emotionally stronger because we are becoming more Christlike.

The ultimate goal of righteous self-government is to live in such a way that we have nothing to hide, that if everyone knew us for what we really are, there would be no shame. Such self-confidence epitomizes spiritual and psychological strength. And, in actuality, when the earth is in its "sanctified and immortal state," that is exactly how things will be. All creation will be known as it really is. "This earth . . . will be made like unto crystal and will be a Urim and Thummim to the inhabitants who dwell thereon" (D&C 130:9). We know that the Urim and Thummim give revelatory powers to the righteous; thus, the inhabitants of the earth will know each other for what they are. Nothing will be hidden, and there will be nothing to hide. Imagine what life would be like if we did not fear others' knowing who we truly are because we ourselves approve of who we are. What liberating power such congruence has. We become free of pretense, free of the need to avoid what we fear about ourselves because there is nothing to fear. Attaining that congruence is part of our psychological and spiritual development, and it requires resolve and commitment to change things for the better. The process is an intensely personal one. Others can tell us or show us what to do, but ultimately we each have to do it for ourselves, by ourselves—but with the potential companionship of the Spirit—and in our own time and way.

CHAPTER TWO

....

A LEAP OF FAITH

IT WAS A STRANGE TIME TO BE DISCONTENT. Certainly nobody else was. And why should they be? They were all busy enjoying an exquisite clam chowder and sipping white wine in what could safely be called one of the most pleasing settings in New Hampshire. It was a fall day, but the warmth of the sun blunted the chill in the air. Nature was at her best. The fall colors were unusually radiant, even by New England standards. The sky over the yacht harbor was bright blue, and puffy white clouds floated about, casting their shadows on the brilliant fall colors below. And the clam chowder—well, it was just terrific, even without the white wine.

Actually, I didn't want to be thinking about spiritual discontent any more than those around me did. It all started when a very elegant and sophisticated woman caught my eye. She was wearing suede shoes that matched her sweater and cap. Very stylish. Even chic. It's remarkable how money and a carefully cultivated air of dignity can transform a perfectly harmless sixty-year-old woman into such a stately creature. But imposing she was. Everybody noticed. The waiters moved a little faster than usual. The hostess behaved with more deference than necessary. The prospect of a big tip was clearly on their minds. The other patrons seemed to notice her, too. If you watched carefully, you could catch them stealing a curious glance in her direction whenever it seemed safe to do so.

Regrettably for me, her party was seated at the table right next to mine. She spoke rather loudly, and I soon found myself listening. I shouldn't have, because that's when the trouble began. The first thing I noticed was how she dominated the conversation with comments about her recent trip to Europe to shop for Belgian linens and Bavarian cut glass just for a weekend party. Those at her table appeared enthusiastically attentive, nodding frequently with the same politeness as the waiters. But the thin veil of interest did not conceal the genuine boredom lurking beneath the surface. It was so obvious, yet she never noticed.

As I listened, I began to understand. Everything was not as it had first appeared. It gradually became apparent that this woman of such obvious wealth and distinction found it necessary to advertise her status to impress her luncheon friends. But why? They already knew of her high social and financial status. (Everybody in the room already knew!) Yet she boasted on. I was fascinated.

It occurred to me that this woman, who, on the outside, seemed to have so much, really had very little on the inside. Placing so much importance on appearance was her way of hiding the emptiness just behind the impressive front. Regardless of wealth, talent, or vivacious personality, in the absence of internal substance, the soul is bound to remain impoverished. And that which feeds the soul—true friends, self-acceptance, and spiritual depth—are not usually found in an environment that favors shallow appearances.

As I listened, I wondered if I dared find a way to introduce myself and simply tell this friendless person in disguise what I understood about Jesus. Preposterous, I thought. She would dismiss me with the same reflexive indifference as she would an annoying fly on her croissant. Worse yet, she might indignantly have me removed. We were truly strangers, and talking over clam chowder wouldn't help bridge the real gap that separated us. There is a curious irony in this story. Had I been fashionably dressed and selling costly yachts, I could have easily arranged to dine with this woman and her companions. A similar invitation could have been arranged if I had been selling stocks, bonds, jewels, or imported wines. And the irony? She already had all of those things. She would gladly have talked with me about what she already had and didn't need; but what she needed most and didn't have couldn't be talked about at all.

Maybe she just didn't know any other way to act. Behavioral scientists would say she was a product of social conditioning. Theologians would probably call her prideful, maybe even sinful. The poor would envy her security. Other striving socialites would say anything just to gain her favor. But it doesn't really matter what you call it because it all boils down to the same thing: she was motivated by worldly desires, which, when satisfied, would bring no satisfaction.

Many of us, like the elegant woman from New Hampshire, have unwittingly been conditioned socially to value things that are pleasing to the body but unsatisfying to the soul. This conditioning occurs so naturally that most of us hardly even notice it—which is what makes it so dangerous. Such subtle influences make it no small task to learn to do the right things for the right reasons, to remember that "man looketh on the outward appearance, but the Lord looketh on the heart" (1 Samuel 16:7).

Social conditioning teaches us to parade our accomplishments and hide our personal struggles. Virtually all of us do it. This tendency is evident even in some of the most benign human rituals. Consider, for example, the traditional Christmas letters many of us receive from family members and friends:

"Dear Folks,

"This holiday season we are getting an earlier start on our Christmas cards and hope that you are still on speaking terms with us.

"George was promoted to Associate Dean at the college, and his new assignment keeps him very busy. Before the change was made official, however, he was able to complete his latest book, which will be published in about four months. He is very happy to have it finished. He is now in his third year of service as stake president and continues to consult with several large corporations nationally and internationally. Last year, his consulting work took him to the Orient and Europe on two different occasions. They were very enjoyable trips. The highlight of the year was a family trip to Europe while George consulted with one of his companies. We visited all of Germany and Austria, and it was a wonderful experience for all of us to share.

"Jerry is now fourteen and is quarterback on the football team and guard on the basketball team. He was ordained a teacher last month. He received state recognition for his SAT math score as a participant in Duke University's talent searches. He also won second place at his school in the American Junior High Math exam . . . "

Nothing is said about gratitude for family blessings or about the significance of the birth of Christ and his mission, even though this is a Christmas letter from active Latter-day Saints. Success, status, and not-so-subtle boasting prevail in this example of cultural conditioning negatively influencing spiritual sensitivity.

The members of this family are not evildoers or hypocrites. They have most certainly given long hours of service to others as well as made every effort to be active and worthy Church members—which is exactly the point. Everyone needs some form of approval. The struggle is to keep that need from interfering when our motives should be spiritual. Another typical example is a testimony meeting in which someone stands and expresses his or her feelings simply to get attention. The meeting then becomes a forum for self-expression and attention getting rather than an opportunity for testimony building, yet the person speaking is unable to tell the difference.

OUR BOTHERSOME HUMAN NATURE

Our susceptibility to the allure of worldly wealth and recognition is nothing new. With his usual incisiveness and candor, Hugh Nibley said: "We know what Zion is, we know what Babylon is, we know that the two can never mix, and we know that Latter-day Saints, against the admonition of their leaders, have always tried to mix them. How is that done? By the use of rhetoric—'The art of making true things seem false and false things seem true by the use of words.' The trick is to appear rich as the result of being good." He described man's obsession with wealth as "no mere red thread running through the scriptures but the broad highway of history" (*Approaching Zion*, vol. 9 of *The Collected Works of Hugh Nibley*, ed. Don E. Norton [Salt Lake City: Deseret Book and F.A.R.M.S., 1989], xv–xvi, 59).

The scriptures are equally clear in their warnings. For example, Moroni tells us: "Behold, I speak unto you as if ye were present, and yet ye are not. But behold, Jesus Christ hath shown you unto me, and I know your doing. And I know that ye do walk in the pride of your hearts. . . . For behold, ye do love money, and your substance, and your fine apparel, and the adorning of your churches, more than ye love the poor and the needy, the sick and the afflicted" (Mormon 8:35–37).

Our bothersome human nature has always put us at risk of compromising our spiritual values for secular gain. But wealth isn't the real problem. It is only the most obvious symptom and symbol of a preoccupation with immediate pleasure, recognition, and status that are so typical of the natural man. Where material blessings were once thankfully acknowledged as the by-products of obeying the Lord, they have now become an end in themselves. Mankind now seems to bypass obedience and head straight for the material blessing. No longer is it obedience but wealth that is valued. We seem to have forgotten that the earth's abundance was created to sustain and edify man. It appears that the function of mortal abundance has been altered from saving edification to mere gratification.

Material things can gratify in two different ways. The use of such possessions as boats or other recreational vehicles brings immediate pleasure. There is nothing wrong with that kind of gratification when it is balanced with gratitude and giving and when it is not perceived as the most important activity in our lives. The second form of gratification is more problematic: when we derive gratification from what we think such possessions represent—success, status, or superiority. When we turn material blessings into symbols of pride, the edifying benefit of those blessings is lost.

This pride is not limited to material things. It manifests itself in every behavior that is motivated by a need to impress others, gain their approval, or appear better than those around us. When we represent ourselves as something we are not in order to gain attention or social acceptance, our motives are outwardly grounded, prompted by attempts to seek gratification that is neither psychologically nor spiritually edifying.

Disrupting this tendency to be motivated by outward things requires us to discriminate between what we do for others' acceptance and what we do for the Lord's. That level of introspection can be frightening. In our practice as therapists, it is not uncommon, particularly in groups, to hear patients acknowledge their fear and reluctance to take the therapeutic step of looking at themselves as they really are. Many have likened themselves to the film character Indiana Jones, who, in one of his adventures, must find the Holy Grail in order to save his father's life. But before the hero can possess the grail, he must traverse a deep chasm with no apparent bridge upon which to cross, only a clue that speaks of a leap—in the words of Indiana, a leap of faith. With one foot on the edge of the chasm, he pauses, unable to move. But hearing his father's groans of pain, he fights his fear and steps out into the void to what appears to be his death. Miraculously, he lands on a narrow bridge of rock that was obscured by the cliffs behind it. He crosses the chasm, wins the grail, and saves his father. Many of our patients are not so lucky, however. They stand frozen with one foot extended, unable to go any further. What they cannot see, they cannot believe exists.

Scrutinizing ourselves and evaluating our motives require a similar leap of faith. We must believe that looking at ourselves with complete candor is worth the risk of the unpleasant things we may well learn. The only way we can improve is to confront in ourselves what needs to be improved. Thus, the first step toward becoming righteously self-governing is to scrutinize our own actions and motives: what are our real reasons for doing the things we do?

CHAPTER THREE

BECOMING RIGHTEOUSLY SELF-GOVERNING

BECOMING RIGHTEOUSLY SELF-GOVERNING means doing the right thing for the right reason, particularly when faced with opposition. The person who is righteously self-governing is motivated by neither duty nor "shoulds" nor compliance with the will or wishes of others. Rather, the spiritual self responds to the challenges of mortality as a righteous child of God.

Righteous self-government is based on acknowledging to ourselves and the Lord any unrighteousness and then striving to overcome it. Making that acknowledgment is an act of choosing that allows us to break free from our mortal foibles instead of denying their existence while we painfully suppress them. We can grit our teeth and by sheer willpower restrain ourselves from un-Christlike actions, but that is a far cry from the change of heart that roots out all evil and makes us like Christ (see Alma 5:14). One is a mental process that behavioral conditioning may accomplish. The other is a spiritual transformation that only the Spirit can inspire. Both may outwardly appear the same, but the difference between them is vast. Much as painting over a crack in the wall differs from repairing and then painting it, righteous self-government goes beyond the cosmetic appeal of mere restraint to demand that what is inside be just as pleasing. Elder Dean L. Larsen described the need to focus on inner qualities rather than on outward indicators:

"The real power in the kingdom of God is not represented in outwardly observable things. Its strength is in the quality of the lives of its members. It is in the depth of their purity, their charity, their faith, their integrity, and their devotion to truth. . . .

" . . . In God's kingdom, power is not equated with body count nor with outward routine compliance with prescribed performances. It is found in those quiet uncharted acts of love, obedience, and Christian service which may never come to the attention of official leadership, but which emulate the ministry of the Lord himself" ("The Strength of the Kingdom Is Within," *Ensign*, Nov. 1981, 25–27).

Righteous self-government suggests that a person's goodness is defined by something more than behavior alone. Good conduct is important, but good conduct that is a genuine expression of spiritual substance is infinitely more important. The scriptures regularly instruct us to seek the Spirit, and then good works will follow naturally. For example, Alma states, "And see that ye have faith, hope, and charity, and then ye will always abound in good works" (Alma 7:24). Similarly, Paul's sermon on charity leaves little doubt about the importance of motives in Christian conduct: "And though I bestow all my goods to feed the poor, and though I give my body to be burned, and have not charity, it profiteth me nothing" (1 Corinthians 13:3). Medieval author Thomas à Kempis said, "Without love, the outward work is of no value; but whatever is done out of love, be it never so little, is wholly fruitful. For God regards the greatness of the love that prompts a man, rather than the greatness of his achievement" (in John S.

Tanner, "Not a Mind without a Soul," *BYU Today,* Mar. 1991, 27).

The role of motives in Christian service is illustrated by the following experiences of two dedicated Relief Society presidents. One filled her calling out of love; the other, by a need for acceptance. Despite the similarity in their outward behavior, the difference in their motives affected these two women.

Martha's hesitation at the church door was scarcely noticeable, but it was there nonetheless. Was it only six months ago that she used to go bounding into the meetinghouse, hardly able to wait for her long Sunday to begin? It seemed more like a million years since the ward members had raised their hands to thank her for her three years of service as Relief Society president. Three years of visiting the sick, filling out food orders, consoling the bereaved, and fighting with the Primary for women to staff her organization.

She had tried hard to do a good job. She had tended to the needs of others carefully. She had made time for others when there really wasn't any time. She thought she'd done the job she was supposed to do, but then she was released. A month went by, then two, then three. Where were the eager hands that she shook on Sundays? Where were the compassionate when she was ill?

Martha had tried hard to meet everyone's expectations. Didn't she deserve the same attention she had given? What was the use of knocking herself out for three years when it was evident nobody cared? With each passing Sunday, the questions grew greater and greater as her exuberance to attend church grew less and less.

Helen sighed as she closed the door to the bishop's office behind her. After three years as the ward Relief Society president, she wasn't sure whether she should laugh or cry. It seemed a burden had been lifted from her, but she also felt a heaviness of heart, knowing that there were still so many others to serve. A silent resolve filled her as she stepped outside into the cool evening air; one calling was no longer hers, but the desire to serve still was.

The weeks went by, and she was once again absorbed into the bustle of an active, busy ward. It came as no surprise that the hellos and inquiring smiles decreased in direct proportion to the time that had passed since her release. She was a sister in a ward full of sisters.

Though she didn't want to admit it, she found it more difficult to tap into the spiritual strength that had once been so accessible to her. And though she couldn't say she felt hurt, it somehow disappointed her to realize that much of the way people had treated her was more in response to her calling than it was to the woman who filled it. But those weren't serious problems. She had learned much. The spiritual initiative was now hers, and when she took it, the results were satisfying. Service didn't stop when a calling did. Relationships with the sick and elderly grew stronger and more meaningful as simple love became the sole motivation for her visits. In the absence of requirement, personal desire to serve flourished. There were times when an undeniable feeling that she could only describe as "rightness" crept over her. When it was there, she felt an overwhelming sense of gratitude; when it wasn't, somehow that seemed all right, too.

Both presidents filled their callings in much the same way. They were conscientious in their duties, sensitive to the needs of others, and highly motivated to serve. Yet when they were released, one became withdrawn and disappointed, the other more loving and demonstrative. What made the difference? Motives.

Although observable behavior provides many good clues to the quality of a person, it is the intent of the behavior that counts the most. Helen was primarily motivated by the love she had for those she served. Martha required external approval and reinforcement for her efforts. Equally important, Helen found her efforts intrinsically satisfying, whereas Martha was satisfied only when others noticed what she did. Good deeds are important, but in themselves they are insufficient. Good works born of a good heart matter the most.

A THREE-LEGGED STOOL

Righteous self-government, like a three-legged stool, has three supporting elements. Each must be sturdy in its own right and balance with the other two for maximum strength. The three supports of righteous self-government are identity, congruence, and autonomy. The sturdiness of the three is never more important than when they are burdened with the weight of temptation and opposition. If they waver and break, righteous self-government fails. But if the three supports bear the weight and remain standing, then doing the right things for the right reasons is possible, even in the face of conflict and difficulty.

The Savior's life exemplified the three supporting elements of righteous self-government. The events of the Savior's return to his home in Galilee help us define those three terms: *identity, congruence,* and *autonomy.* On the Sabbath, he entered the synagogue and, while reading from the scriptures, undeniably declared his godhood. That must have been a lonely moment. To risk being known as we truly are without the assurance of being accepted can be frightening. But the Savior went one step further. He revealed his divine nature, knowing full well that the response would be hostile. Yet could he have done anything else? He never denied his divine origins. Regardless of time, place, or audience, his identity was constant and consistent. Individual *identity,* then, is the first element of righteous self-government.

Elder James E. Talmage tells us that the passages of scripture the Savior read were viewed as specifically referring to the Messiah. There was no misunderstanding, only mistrust and incredulity. "And all bare him witness, and wondered at the gracious words which proceeded out of his mouth. And they said, Is not this Joseph's son?" (Luke 4:22). His magnificent pronouncement was too difficult for his countrymen to equate with the son of Joseph, someone they had known as no different from themselves. Recognizing their skepticism, the Savior reminded them that no prophet is accepted in his own country. He also discerned their curiosity and their desire for him to replicate the miracles which had been reported from Capernaum. Once again using the scriptures, he challenged their need for him to prove himself, recounting ancient times when Gentiles and others the Jews considered beneath them had been blessed by God while the chosen people were ignored. According to Talmage, "Then great was their wrath. Did He dare to class them with Gentiles and lepers? Were they to be likened unto despised unbelievers, and that too by the son of the village carpenter, who had grown from childhood in their community? Victims of diabolical rage, they seized the Lord and took Him to the brow of the hill on the slopes of which the town was built, determined to avenge their wounded feelings by hurling Him from the rocky cliffs" (*Jesus the Christ* [Salt Lake City: Deseret Book, 1949], 180).

The unpretentious power of the Lord's words that day extended into his behavior as well. The crowd's vicious desire to murder him was met by a quiet but unstoppable retreat from their midst. Certainly, in his omniscience, the Lord knew that he would not be welcomed by his former neighbors in Nazareth. Yet he returned there to do his Father's bidding. Furthermore, according to Matthew's account of the rejection in Nazareth, all outward appearances indicate that Jesus' attempts to preach in his home failed. "And he did not many mighty works there because of their unbelief" (Matthew 13:58).

We see another characteristic of righteous self-government in the Savior's willingness to return to his boyhood home with full foreknowledge of the crowd's hostility and his own peril: righteous behavior is never motivated by assurances of a positive outcome. Righteous behavior is inherently motivating notwithstanding outcome. Righteously self-governed individuals act to maintain harmony between personal goodness within and good works without. That is enough reward. No public success can ever eclipse the personal contentment of harmony between self and God. Consequently, like Christ, the righteously self-governed present themselves on the outside in a way that simply and consistently reflects what they are on the inside. Deep personal *congruence,* then, is the second element of righteous self-government.

The Savior's candor and honesty with which he presented himself to everyone gives us additional insight into righteous self-government. Many times we are willing to adjust ourselves to current conditions in a bid to reduce our own discomfort. By acting, talking, and even dressing a certain way, we hope to increase our chances of winning acceptance or at least to reduce our chances of drawing negative attention to ourselves. The Lord never compromised principle and therefore never compromised himself in order to be found more acceptable to others. He never acted out of fear. On the contrary, in Nazareth, as later in Pilate's palace and in Gethsemane and on Calvary, during the most difficult and trying moments when all were against him, he demonstrated his godly ability to be self-directing and motivated by principle rather than by pressure. By removing himself from the religious, social, and political influences of those around him, he showed in his independence the depth of his dependence on one, and only one, other: God the Father. The third element of righteous self-government, then, is personal *autonomy*, with dependence on God through our Savior, Jesus Christ.

IMITATORS OF RIGHTEOUS SELF-GOVERNMENT

Even the most convincing imitators of righteous self-government all have the same fatal flaw: their motives and rewards come from external sources, not internal ones. As a consequence, their outward behavior is seldom an autonomous, congruent expression of their internal/eternal identity. Two common manifestations of this deception are The Dependent and The True Believer.

The Dependent is not easy to recognize. Outwardly such a person may have a pleasing and conforming personality, but just beneath the surface lurks a nagging insecurity that drives the conformity. Consequently, dependency may look pleasing, but it is seldom healthy. In fact, it is at the core of some common emotional and spiritual problems.

The term *dependency* refers to being in a position in which a person's behavior is overly influenced or even determined by another. Though we are all influenced by those around us, dependent people constantly adjust their behavior to increase their chances of gaining the approval and acceptance of others. Dependent people try to be what others want them to be. That is what makes this personality style so dangerous: it is guided almost exclusively by external influences, whereas the principal components of spiritual and psychological strength are internal.

The price of this personality style is high. Dependent people do not learn to behave in ways that will allow them to feel self-respect and self-approval because they are so busy catering to the expectations of others. They forsake countless opportunities for emotional and spiritual growth by denying the reality of their own thoughts and feelings so as not to upset those whose favor they are constantly courting. The following story illustrates how this behavior pattern that appears so pleasing to others can in reality be individually destructive.

"Ask Stella. She'll do it," was a comment made frequently in bishopric meetings, PTA meetings, and in family reunion committees. If you asked anybody in Stella's ward to pick out a person who was humble, helpful, and happy, few would fail to name Stella—if not first, then surely within three tries. Stella was a consistent beneficiary of the adage: "If you want something done, get a busy person to do it." Not only did she serve as Primary in-service leader but she was on the ward activities committee, and every time there was a wedding, funeral, or birth in the ward, someone called on Stella to help with a shower, a meal, or baby-sitting. Every assignment was accepted, and every request granted.

Stella's family was also very active. There were the children's music lessons, baseball games, Scouts, Mutual, and who could forget the clogging? Certainly not Stella. She attended each child's every recital, game, and program. Few other parents showed as much support for their children. Bart, Stella's husband, always had clean, pressed shirts, lunch packed in the morning, and dinner on time at night. When he had to work late, Stella understood. When the elders quorum had a steak fry or welfare assignment, Stella always helped Bart with his responsibilities as quorum president.

Yes, Stella was reliable. She was supportive. She was helpful. And she was dependent. In rendering charity at church, support in the family, and service in the community, Stella's dependency was almost impossible to detect. Trying to please others took the guise of charitable acts. Avoiding the disappointment of her children masqueraded as parental support. Bids for acceptance were camouflaged by volunteering for neighborhood projects. At church meetings and social gatherings, Stella laughed at jokes she didn't like, nodded her head in approval of opinions she didn't agree with, and when asked to voice her own thoughts, simply parroted the prevailing attitude. At home, she quietly tolerated Bart's periodic outbursts of anger and verbal abuse, cleaned up after the kids when they ignored her requests to clean up after themselves, and rarely called up a friend to do something with her out of fear that she might not be home if somebody needed her.

Stella was also miserable. It was a quiet sort of misery, though, one difficult to detect because Stella was so good at hiding it. She had also perfected her ability to cover what she truly thought and to stifle what she truly wanted. As a matter of fact, she had denied her own thoughts and feelings for so long that it had become almost impossible for Stella to discern the difference between her own desires and the wishes of others.

Where along the line Stella had lost herself in the needs and wants of others is difficult to know. Somewhere, early in life, she had learned that doing what she was asked to do minimized conflict with others and maximized acceptance from them. People like people who do things for them. Leaders like people who accept assignments and follow through with them. There is so much less awkwardness and embarrassment in saying yes than in saying no. But there are many hazards in relying on such approval and acceptance. Limited identity, congruity, and autonomy result in our personal wishes being constantly sacrificed for those of others. Consequently, how important and influential can our identity be? When we are unwilling or incapable of expressing what we are, our identities go unexercised and, as a result, atrophy.

Stella wanted to say no to the last request (at ten o'clock at night) for three dozen muffins for the Scout breakfast fundraiser the next morning. But what she felt inside was shoved aside by her need for external approval. She was thinking and feeling one thing while saying and doing another. On a very fundamental level, Stella knew she was doing what appeared to be the right thing but for the wrong reason. And that incongruity generated shame, shame that she hid from herself and others by continually doing over and over again the very thing that produced the shame in the first place: saying yes when she meant no. As long as she did that, she had no self-approval, no internally generated praise. She therefore had to seek it on the outside from others—the very action that caused her feelings of shame.

Autonomy? Stella was like a mirror. Her behavior reflected

the behavior of those around her. Her own desires were swallowed up in the desires of others. Stella responded as she thought others wanted her to. She was tethered to her ward, her family, her friends. Autonomy could not influence her life while the influence of others exceeded the influence she exerted on herself. As long as she was a prisoner of others' approval, she would never gain approval of herself. Righteous self-government cannot exist in the presence of the nagging need for approval from others.

The True Believer is a prime example of the automatic and often mindless conformity that develops when people seek personal security through their activities in important organizations instead of through meaningful personal development (see Eric Hoffer, *The True Believer* [New York: Perennial Library, 1989]). Generally speaking, True Believers tend to be disaffected, discontented, and frustrated. They have a sense of hopelessness about the present, feel unable to do anything to change their future, and experience continual feelings of worthlessness and helplessness. They lack a sense of spiritual or psychological identity and tend to be governed more by external circumstances than by their own internal thoughts and feelings.

Because of their deep sense of powerlessness, True Believers routinely affiliate with groups that have a cause, whether social movements, religious organizations, or political parties. The goal of joining any of them is usually to add meaning and purpose to the True Believers' lives, meaning and purpose that they have failed to acquire on their own. Though the groups vary, some common characteristics of affiliation are easily identifiable. The group gives its members a sense of importance and power, generally because it is based on a potent idea or it has an infallible or charismatic leader or some other unique claim to fame. True Believers come to believe that through their affiliation with their new cause there is hope for them; their newfound sense of importance depends entirely on the importance of the group. Their loyalty to the group and its teachings becomes complete and unwavering. With time, their sense of identity and personal value comes exclusively from their affiliation with and conformity to the cause. Their conformity is, in the truest sense, mindless.

Ed was rock-solid. His devotion to the Church and his family seemed unwavering and undeniable. He proudly displayed his "R U LDS" bumper stickers on both family cars. Church meetings were never missed, family home evenings were always held, and ward social activities were faithfully attended. There was no question that Ed was loyal, dutiful, and obedient.

To the casual observer, he appeared to be an active member of the Church with a strong testimony, if just a little rigid in the way he expressed himself. On closer examination, however, Ed's participation seemed more a cookie cutter replica of something someone else had said than actions motivated by a genuine testimony that could stand by itself. Hearing him bear his testimony was almost like listening to a broken record. He relied on trite phrases and cliches rather than using his own words to express his knowledge and faith.

Luckily, Ed had a hidden asset. It was a little unusual, to be sure, but it was an asset nevertheless. Discontent deep within warned him that something was wrong. He used outward activities, programs, and publications to satisfy his discontent. But it wouldn't go away until his cravings for power and belonging were satisfied by his own emotional and spiritual adequacy.

The sad irony of the True Believers' situation is that in their efforts to improve their own spiritual status, they turn their attention completely outward and abandon the inner self, which is the only instrument there is for achieving lasting spiritual and psychological health and happiness. With the abandonment of identity, autonomy also disappears, because True Believers' beliefs and behaviors are based on what they think others want them to think and feel. And unless their inner discontent becomes stronger than the need to conform, there can be no congruence.

Although both The Dependent and The True Believer appear to be actively and righteously self-governing, there is little similarity between their lives and the life of the Savior. Further examination of the concepts of identity, congruence, and autonomy will show that doing the right things for the right reasons is the only way to become truly Christlike.

WHO AM I?

OUR SEARCH FOR IDENTITY IS AS OLD AS ADAM and Eve's first communications with the Lord after they were driven out of the Garden of Eden. Through prayer they maintained their relationship with Heavenly Father, reinforcing their identities as his son and daughter (see Moses 5:4–5).

The knowledge of our divine origins has waxed and waned over the several millennia that people have inhabited the earth. The more that modern thinking replaces the spiritual foundation of our identity with a secular view, the greater our need to understand who we really are. That understanding is often difficult to come by because each of us is composed of many different parts, some of which may appear contradictory.

A paramount task of mortality is to order and regulate correctly the different facets of the self. The more complicated life is, the more likely we are to fall into the trap of perceiving our identity less in relationship to God and more in relationship to the transient aspects of mortality: how much we produce, how much we have, or our position on the social and professional ladders of the society that surrounds us. Without a clear sense of self, it is impossible for us to become righteously self-governing.

SELF-INVENTORY OF PERSONAL IDENTITY

Identity is knowing ourselves as only we are capable of knowing. Gaining that knowledge requires an honest assessment and understanding of ourselves. The following questions will help you assess your own self-knowledge.

SCALE

> 1 = This statement is true of me MOST of the time.
> 2 = This statement is true of me MUCH of the time.
> 3 = This statement is true of me SOME of the time.
> 4 = This statement is true of me ALMOST NONE of the time.

QUESTIONS

____ 1. I am emancipated from my parents and have become my own person.

____ 2. At this time in my life, I have a deep sense of meaning and purpose that gives me direction.

____ 3. My behavior is usually an expression of my most important values.

____ 4. I seldom let others influence me more than I like to admit.

____ 5. Most of the time I am the kind of person I always wanted to be.

____ 6. I am aware of the times when my actions do not reflect what I truly think and feel.

____ 7. My behavior is directed more by my internal compass than by the opinions of those around me.

____ 8. My spiritual self is alive and dependable; I rely regularly on its influence.

_____ 9. I have a deep sense of right and wrong, upon which I base important decisions.

_____ 10. My religious conviction is more a product of my own private searching than it is of social conditioning, conformity, or family pressure.

Your score may be as low as ten or as high as forty. The lower the score, the more likely you are to have a clear sense of individual identity.

SPIRITUAL IDENTITY

A number of scriptures attest that we existed before mortality. Abraham tells us:

"Now the Lord had shown unto me, Abraham, the intelligences that were organized before the world was; and among all these there were many of the noble and great ones;

"And God saw these souls that they were good, and he stood in the midst of them, and he said: These I will make my rulers; for he stood among those that were spirits, and he saw that they were good; and he said unto me: Abraham, thou art one of them; thou wast chosen before thou wast born" (Abraham 3:22–23).

Other scriptures make the same point. In Doctrine and Covenants the Lord discusses our "creation before the world was made" (D&C 49:17). The Lord tells us that "man was also in the beginning with God" (D&C 93:29). The Prophet Joseph Smith commented on the eternal nature of our spirits when he said, "There never was a time when there were not spirits; for they are co-equal [co-eternal] with our Father in heaven" (*Teachings of the Prophet Joseph Smith*, sel. Joseph Fielding Smith [Salt Lake City: Deseret Book, 1976], 353).

Our eternal identity consists of intelligence that was never created, combined with a part that was spiritually created by our Heavenly Father. These two parts compose our eternal identity, which existed before we were born and accompanied us into mortality. Each individual's eternal identity is different from any other eternal identity. It contributes to our earthly personality, and it is influenced by earthly experiences. It is also the enduring, fundamental self that can transcend circumstance, culture, race, genetics, or other temporal and temporary influences. It is the essence of who we are and of what we may become.

PSYCHOLOGICAL IDENTITY

One distinct attribute that separates human beings from all other forms of life is our ability to reflect on our own existence and, out of that self-awareness, make individual choices that define the purpose and direction our lives will follow. This capacity for self-awareness and choice makes psychological identity possible. Our values, which motivate what we think and feel, give our identities substance.

Ironically, our capacity for self-awareness and individual identity can create as much personal distress as it can happiness. If we truly believe that our happiness is largely the result of our choices, it follows that our unhappiness is the result of our failure to choose wisely. Our awareness of our own influence in creating the life we experience can be a source of considerable distress, particularly for those who struggle to find meaning in lifestyles that have no eternal meaning.

IDENTITY IS THE SOURCE OF MEANING

Our spiritual and psychological identities are fed by strikingly similar nutrients: interest and concern for the well-being of something or someone other than ourselves. Extending ourselves beyond our own self-interests appears to play a crucial role in our finding meaning and purpose in what we do and who we are. One way to see the breadth and depth of this influence is to study people who have either a distinct or a vague sense of meaning in their lives. Factual information on this topic is limited, but what is available is revealing. For example, renowned psychiatrist Viktor Frankl interviewed sixty university students after they attempted suicide. The reason given by 85 percent of the students for their suicide attempt was that life seemed meaningless. Ironically, nearly all of them were socially active, were doing well in school, and had good relationships with their families. Their suicide attempts were driven not by chronic failure, crisis, alcoholism, or isolation but by an impoverished sense of personal meaning and purpose (see *The Unheard Cry for Meaning: Psychotherapy and Humanism* [New York: Simon & Schuster, 1978]).

Similarly, a professor of psychiatry at Stanford University, Irvin Yalom, offered the following conclusions about the role that a sense of meaning plays in our lives: first, a lack of personal meaning and purpose is related to emotional and behavioral problems of all types and varieties. Generally speaking, the less clear the sense of personal meaning and identity, the greater the personal and social problems. Second, having religious beliefs and values seems to be related to having a positive sense of meaning and purpose. Third, having values that include an interest in the welfare of others is related to a positive sense of meaning and purpose. And fourth, having a clear sense of life goals is associated with a positive sense of self and purpose (see *Existential Human Psychotherapy* [New York: Basic Books, 1980]).

Frankl made similar observations much earlier and in an entirely different setting—in the Nazi death camp at Auschwitz. The circumstances couldn't have been more dire or despicable, which is what makes Frankl's observations so striking. He found that those who were willing to help others or had a vision of some future purpose had a better chance of surviving their ordeal in the concentration camp than did those who had no sense of mission or meaning in life. Frankl spent the better part of his professional life deeply immersed in the problem of understanding how we acquire meaning in our personal lives. He created a unique theory for enhancing human development called logotherapy, which means, literally, "healing through meaning." Frankl suggests that a sense of meaning and purpose is usually the result of being engaged in activities that transcend our own personal interests. Accordingly, he notes, our search for meaning is a primary human motive from which our values and ideals are formulated and for which we live, and, if necessary, for which we are willing to die (see Viktor E. Frankl, *Man's Search for Meaning* [New York: Washington Square Press, 1984]).

There is a strong similarity between such conclusions and the essential message of the scriptures that service to others is a source of personal meaning. The truth is, much of the way we view ourselves is determined by the way we treat others. Ironically, most of us have been taught just the opposite, that the way others treat us will determine how we feel about ourselves. Psychologist Rollo May suggested that being overly sensitive to external influence creates "hollow people" who have little understanding of who they are or what they actually feel. He reported one person who described himself as a collection of mirrors, reflecting only what everyone expected of him (see *Man's Search for Himself* [New York: Dell, 1953]).

Similarly, others have suggested that alienation from self is the result of developing a life determined by others rather than a life based on one's own inner experiences. Latter-day prophets have expressed the same view in stronger terms. For example, President David O. McKay said: "Mere compliance with the word of the Lord, without a corresponding inward desire, will avail but little. Indeed, such outward actions and pretending phrases may disclose hypocrisy, a sin that Jesus most vehemently condemned" (*Gospel Ideals* [Salt Lake City: Deseret Book, 1953], 382).

The underlying point of these prophetic and scientific observations is the same: it is spiritually and psychologically hazardous for our outward behavior to be anything other than a natural expression of our internal identity. That congruence requires us to have a reasonably clear and accurate sense of our spiritual and psychological self.

The discovery of personal meaning coincides with the discovery of our identity. Attending to our internal/eternal identity is best understood as a process rather than an objective we eventually reach. Furthermore, the development of identity is not only a process but an evolving process. What we do today will influence what we do tomorrow, and what we do tomorrow will influence what we think is possible the day after. Each step along the way can alter the next day's path, allowing only fleeting glimpses of the final destination because our understanding of what is possible for us keeps changing even as we change.

Enhancing Individual Identity

The following is a variation of an exercise we use at professional workshops. We have found that doing the activity feels much different from just reading about it. And we have learned that it is quite helpful to do this exercise with someone with whom we can talk openly and honestly when we are finished.

First, you should find a place that is comfortable and where you can be free of interruptions. With eyes closed, take five minutes to relax. One way of doing that is to breathe deeply and focus on the sensations and rhythm of breathing.

Next, silently identify an actual problem situation or a conflict you have had to deal with. It can involve anger, intimacy, fear, loneliness, authority figures, recurring temptations, or any personal weakness. Anything will do as long as the situation was difficult at the time. Then, with the situation clearly in mind, recall it in as much detail as possible. Observe your own behavior, speech, pressures, fears, and other emotions. Once you are satisfied that the recollection is reasonably complete, replay the incident in your mind three times as though it were a movie, studying yourself carefully each time. With the images clearly in mind, write down as specifically as possible three things you saw yourself do that you wish you hadn't.

Now close your eyes again, and reenter the problem situation. Take yourself right up to the point of the behavior you wish you hadn't engaged in and then stop and ask yourself: "What do I need to do in this situation now so that I will approve of myself later?" Please notice that the question is *not* how desirable, feasible, practical, difficult, or popular the behavior might be. Neither is it whether the behavior will solve or even ease the existing difficulty. Focus only on what you would have to do so you can approve of yourself later, no matter what happens.

Then insert this new, ideal behavior in place of the behavior you originally found objectionable. Replay this new scenario three times, allowing it to change if your thoughts or feelings about it change. Study yourself carefully in each replay.

Conclude the exercise by opening your eyes. Ask yourself the following questions and discuss them with the trustworthy person who did the exercise with you. These questions are intended to help you discern the difference between the voice of your real internal self and the voices of external social influences. The questions will also help you understand why we may have trouble recognizing our internal voice.

1. Am I regularly inclined to turn inward to search for my internal feelings and personal sense of right and wrong in important situations, or do I respond before I am fully aware of how I really think and feel?

2. During this exercise, was I able to suspend myself temporarily from such external influences as seeking success, avoiding fear, pretending, or pleasing others in order to see what my internal self would have me do?

3. If I am unaccustomed to carefully attending to my internal self for direction, have I noticed feeling uncomfortable about what I am doing on some occasions?

4. Would I find it difficult to represent myself consistently the way I really am?

5. What would happen to the quality of my life if I represented myself in ways that were entirely consistent with my real thoughts and feelings, particularly in difficult situations?

Here is Greg's experience. It all started about three years after Greg returned from his mission. Nothing remarkable had happened up to that time. He had elected to live at home. He quickly became financially independent of his parents and bought his own car. All things considered, he pretty much lived his life as he wanted. That was fine with his parents. They were happy he was home and even happier to see him living his own life.

As Greg started thinking about marrying his girlfriend, Fay, he found it perfectly natural to talk with both his parents about his deepest feelings and concerns. There was nothing unusual about these talks because the family had a long history of openness about the things that mattered most to them. The family's ability to talk candidly had always been an important problem-solving tool for everyone, but gradually these conversations changed. Tensions increased between Greg and the rest of the family when they asked him important questions about his plans to marry Fay—questions that included the usual assortment of concerns for newlyweds, such as finances, education, and employment. But Greg found the questions annoying and expressed his disdain by avoiding answering. Though everyone was motivated by concern for Greg and Fay, Greg was not appreciative and became increasingly frustrated in his attempts to talk with his family. Finally, he stopped talking and began to withdraw. Everybody immediately noticed.

Things turned ugly when he was asked about it over dinner one evening. With resounding anger, he announced that he was tired of others trying to run his life, that if he wanted anyone's advice he would ask for it, and that he was upset and disappointed with his entire family. Everybody was stunned. A new and more serious problem emerged. The family stopped trying to talk to Greg about things that mattered. When they

did try, they were met with angry outbursts. Superficial politeness replaced honesty. Something very important had
changed, and nobody quite understood why.

Tensions between Greg and his family accelerated at an
alarming rate. Without any explanation, Fay stopped coming
over to the house. A wedding was planned with no family dialogue whatsoever, and Greg moved out a month before the
wedding. The whole family was not together until the wedding
day, when they met as emotional strangers, with detached
awkwardness replacing feelings of tenderness.

When Greg went through the exercise we previously
described, he was amazed at how he consistently had betrayed
the deepest feelings that came from his real identity. In brief,
Greg came to see that not only had he failed to look inward to
find a sense of personal direction, but he had actually ignored
and opposed his deepest feelings. He identified the three most
important things he did in this problem situation that he
wished he hadn't done:

1. *He felt hurt, but he acted angry.* Greg's feelings were hurt
in two important ways. First, family members raised questions
about his marriage plans that he had overlooked. The implica-
tion of those oversights was clear in Greg's mind: family members did not trust or respect his ability to plan thoroughly. That
possibility hurt his feelings. Second, Greg did not experience
the family support and encouragement he was expecting. That
also hurt his feelings. The actual cause of those hurt feelings is
not crucial; it may or may not have been justified. What is
important is that Greg felt them, and because he felt them, he
had a responsibility to cope with them. But he didn't. Instead,
he tried to cover them up by acting angry. In so doing, he took
a giant step toward creating the very problem he wanted to

avoid and gave his family new reasons to doubt the very thing he was trying to prove—that he could think through his marriage plans with the necessary maturity.

2. *He feared a loss of family support, but he acted indifferent.* Again we see in Greg's behavior a denial of his real feelings in favor of something easier to handle. He feared and actually perceived a loss of support from his family. Again, the issue is not whether this loss was real or imagined but rather that Greg felt it. Instead of respecting his feelings and talking openly about them, he hid them and acted deceptively when he believed his family disapproved. By denying his real feelings to himself and others, he also denied himself the opportunity for meaningful problem solving with those he loved.

3. *When Greg did experience a loss of family support, he acted detached and aloof.* The result was that Greg actually came to feel betrayed by his family at an important time in his life. That hurt him deeply. Again, the issue is not the validity of the feelings but what was done with them. Greg chose to minimize and ignore them. Instead of acknowledging what he was feeling, he acted increasingly detached, aloof, and indifferent. Under such conditions, things could only get worse, and they did.

As you recall, the second part of the exercise required Greg to replace the behavior he objected to with actions he could take in order to approve of himself later, no matter what the result. Greg's response was very perceptive. Without any prompting, he said that he would have looked at his own feelings more honestly and been more open about them with his family. In other words, he would have let his real identity play a more influential role in directing his responses. If he had, he felt that most of the problem would have been avoided. And he was probably right. The family was not opposed to his marrying Fay; they were only opposed to his defensiveness. And Greg learned an important lesson in this exercise because of his courage in facing himself honestly. He saw that he had played a major role in creating the very problem he had originally blamed on others and resented them for. His ability to see that truth was a much more accurate reflection of the qualities of his internal/eternal identity than anything that had happened while he was alienated from it.

Our willingness to honestly examine our own thoughts, feelings, and behaviors and then evaluate them according to what we want to be will greatly enhance our ability to alter and strengthen our sense of who we are. The capacity for honest introspection, for experiencing ourselves as we really are, undergirds all our efforts to cultivate a hardy identity. Following are some additional suggestions for enhancing our identity:

1. *Factor out the fear.* An effective exercise to help us identify our fears is to once again identify an incident in which we did not approve of our thoughts, feelings, or behaviors. Then we determine the degree to which our behavior was motivated by fear—fear of being rejected by others, fear of not getting what we want, fear of embarrassment, fear of failure, fear of success. Next, we take the fear and set it aside. Some people who have done this exercise say that picturing in their minds the fear as a tangible object actually leaving their bodies helps them imagine themselves separating from their fear. With that done, we replay the disapproving scenario as if all our fear were gone. How would the scenario be different in the absence of fear? By factoring out the fear, we are able to see more clearly what we truly want, how we truly want to feel, think, and

behave, and who we truly want to be. Telling the difference between being motivated by fear and being motivated by more positive qualities helps us clarify how we would like to perceive ourselves and be perceived by others, thus strengthening our identity.

2. *Become solution oriented.* Leading therapists are focusing more and more on solutions to individuals' problems rather than on the problems themselves. Historically, a great deal of time was spent in therapy describing problems and then searching for their causes. Many mental health researchers now maintain that it is far more productive to focus on those moments when we think, feel, or behave in ways we approve. Two stories illustrate the differences between these two approaches to the change process:

"A few years back, during that rare year when the Chicago Cubs succeeded in winning their division championship, there was a time when one of the leading hitters was in a slump. Jim Frey, the manager of the team, spotted this hitter in the club-house one day. The hitter, with hopes of improving his performance, was watching films of himself up at bat. Now, you can probably guess what films he chose to watch. Right! He chose films of the times when he was in the slump, when he was striking out and generally doing everything but what he wanted. He, of course, was trying to find out what he was doing wrong so he could correct his mistake. He probably subscribed to the 'What is the cause of the problem?' question. However, you can imagine what he was learning by watching films of slump batting; he was learning in greater and greater detail how to be a slump batter.

"In watching the Winter Olympics a couple of years ago, . . . we noticed the East German women as they were preparing for their run down the hill. As they were sitting in the sled waiting their turn, their eyes were closed. We thought this was rather strange. Then we noticed that with their eyes still closed, they were making strange weaving motions forward, backward, and side to side. We thought this really strange—until the commentator explained that these women were going through a mental preparation of the run. With their eyes closed, they were visualizing going through the run; their body movements were their body responses as they imagined banking off turns and experiencing the acceleration of the run" (John Walter and Jane Peller, *Becoming Solution-Focused in Brief Therapy* [New York: Brunner/Mazel, 1992], 5).

Many of us dwell on our defeats or on the way we do something wrong and exclude what we do right. How we define ourselves to ourselves can be greatly influenced by the proportion of time we spend examining our failures versus successes. A simple way of strengthening our identity is to scan our memory banks periodically for those moments when our self-approval is strong. How would we describe ourselves under those circumstances? How can we direct the same strength, the same understanding, the same positive behavior, in directions where our self-approval is not as great?

One of our clients described herself as unassertive and easily manipulated. She labored over incident after incident in which she felt she had been taken advantage of. After she reported several similar stories, therapy shifted to having her identify times when she felt she had been appropriately assertive. These times, naturally, were fewer and farther between. It was undeniable, however, that she had demonstrated an inner strength that, until then, she had refused to acknowledge in herself. Treatment helped her identify ways that she could transfer those positive characteristics to other situations. She rehearsed in her mind how she would react to threatening situations, replacing her typically unassertive behavior with the assertive actions she had taken at other times. Bringing to the forefront her more admirable traits required her to reassess her self-perception to accommodate her positive characteristics and then to act on them instead.

3. *Redefining failures.* One very important element in successfully overcoming addictive behaviors is to prepare for the inevitable relapses that attend the healing process. How individuals perceive an occasional slip will in large measure determine the degree to which they are able to move forward once again or be inclined to fall back into old behavior patterns. It is absolutely essential to prepare for a relapse so that when it happens it will be considered an isolated incident rather than a commentary on their own fundamental condition. Some therapists prefer to call it a lapse, not a relapse. The attitude must be one of, "Well, I messed up this once. I won't do it again, and it certainly isn't the way I'm going to define myself from here on out." If, on the other hand, individuals perceive their negative behavior as a manifestation of their true selves, the odds are that they will continue to behave in ways that reflect their perception of themselves.

No one is perfect. By avoiding the tendency to define ourselves according to the negative things that we all do occasionally, we will be able to maintain a stronger sense of our identity based on the good things we do. That, in turn, increases the likelihood that we will continue to do good things. Invariably, the weaker or more negative our self-perceptions, the more severe the problems we can experience. On the other hand, the more secure we are in our identity, the greater our ability to cope with problems as they arise. How we choose to define our identity should include an understanding of what it means to be a whole person. Many emotionally troubled people are severe, black-and-white thinkers. If they demonstrate a weakness or behave in self-disapproving ways, they immediately conclude that they are bad. There is little, if any, provision for mistakes. It's all or nothing, black or white. Such individuals have great difficulty understanding that being whole, complete, and real means to contain both positive and negative attributes. In other words, they need to recognize that we have the seeds of perfection planted in us while we are yet imperfect. Our identity must accommodate this mortal phenomenon. The disparity between our real and our ideal self should motivate us to take action to improve rather than overwhelm us into immobility.

To begin the process of cultivating a healthy identity, we must ask ourselves to what degree we should allow our lives to be directed by influences other than our own sense of right and wrong, which emanates from our internal/eternal self. The following story shows that beginning the process of becoming internally directed is the primary step toward establishing a solid identity.

Cindy had been in therapy for several months. Depression, guilt, and anxiety were her chief complaints. They all seemed to be the inevitable consequence of a lifestyle that focused on gaining the approval of others by appearing to be whatever others expected her to be. In a series of particularly difficult sessions, therapy seemed to grind to a halt. She was considering pursuing a career as a means of self-development, but she felt guilty about leaving her children during the day. That her husband didn't approve just made matters worse. She talked endlessly about how she could manage the responsibilities of being both a professional and a homemaker. But no matter how she mentally arranged things, it appeared that she would disappoint someone.

Halfway through one session, the therapist asked her to close her eyes and stop talking. He directed her to eject the influence of all the important people in her life and concentrate on becoming more aware of her own thoughts and feelings. She was to find and listen to her internal voice and answer two questions. First, what did she want to do? Second, did she approve of what she wanted to do? Her answers were to be as free from the influence of guilt or fear as possible.

A surprising thing happened when she turned inward: she did not find the answers she was seeking. Instead, she found only confusion. It was frightening. She had become accustomed, in similar difficult situations, to following the rules and instructions of others. In their absence, she was lost. The sessions that followed focused exclusively on Cindy's increasing her awareness of her own thoughts and feelings about the meaning and direction of her life—the first steps toward learning about her own identity.

Recognizing our own thoughts and feelings is a critical first step in knowing who we are. And knowing who we are helps us define what we truly want out of life. In Cindy's case, as she evaluated her own thoughts and feelings, she realized that she had never really wanted a career. It was an idea she got from a friend who had read a magazine article about working mothers. When external influences exceed the strength of our own internal/eternal identity, we run a much greater risk of getting off the course our lives should follow.

Enhancing Spiritual Identity

Enhancing our spiritual identity is an internal process primarily involving only ourselves and the Lord. There is no such thing as a spiritual recipe, only general guidelines that may precipitate our desire to create the conditions in which our spiritual identity can grow. These conditions include faith, a change of heart, and charity.

Faith. Faith is not so much having something as it is being something. Erich Fromm aptly differentiates between what he calls "having faith" and "being in faith":

"Faith, in the having mode, is the possession of an answer for which one has no rational proof. It consists of formulations created by others, which one accepts because one submits to those others.

"Faith, in the having mode, is a crutch for those who want to be certain, those who want an answer to life without daring to search for it themselves.

"Faith, in the being mode, is . . . an inner orientation, an attitude.

"It is a continuous active process . . . of Christ's eternally being born within ourselves" (*To Have or to Be* [New York: Bantam New Age Books, 1976], 30–31).

Such faith requires us to act from our own understanding and testimony of the Savior and his redeeming grace. In *Lectures on Faith,* the question "What testimony had the immediate descendants of Adam, in proof of the existence of God?" is answered: "The testimony of their father. And after they were made acquainted with his existence, by the testimony of their father, they were dependent upon the exercise of their own faith, for a knowledge of his character, perfections, and attributes"

(Joseph Smith, *Lectures on Faith* [Salt Lake City: Deseret Book, 1985], 27).

There is simply no substitute for individual faith when it comes to knowing the Savior. If and when we are asked whether we recognize the Lord, we assume there will be no one around from whom to seek advice, opinion, or direction. We will have to stand alone, independent of external influence, in our faith, to whatever degree it exists.

The faith to be able to know the Savior is the same faith that will help us know ourselves. The more we seek him out, the greater our sensitivity will be to the inner inklings that accompany our spiritual self. We must literally lose ourselves for Christ's sake in order to find ourselves. When we focus on a power purer and higher than ourselves, we are more capable of transcending the imperfect mortal ego that collects psychological hang-ups and deters us from heeding our healthier spiritual identity.

The faith that motivates us to seek Christ first also motivates us to cultivate our own spiritual identity. We must have sufficient faith to believe that we are capable of discerning promptings from our spiritual self. If we doubt our ability to rely on what we feel, that self-doubt will deter us from undertaking the introspection necessary to seek out our spiritual identity and then attend to it.

To develop the faith to enhance our spiritual identity, we must first ask ourselves, "Do I truly believe that I am innately equipped to discern what is good and bad, right and wrong, by thoughtful and honest introspection?" The key words are *thoughtful* and *honest*. Our introspection must be free from emotional or mental game-playing of any kind before it can be effective. No rationalizations or self-serving emotions are allowed. We must discern the truth regardless of how difficult it may be. Such thoughtful and honest introspection is a way of temporarily suspending selfish preoccupations and preferences in order to turn inward to see how we genuinely feel about something.

We must also recognize that faith is not simply accepting as true that which we have been taught is true. Without individual, rigorous inquiry into the spiritual validity of what has been learned, even the most ardent follower of religious doctrine risks being nothing more than the product of social conditioning. Because faith leaves little room for doubt, many erroneously assume that having faith means never questioning what they believe or take for granted. In reality, true faith does not require us to hide from our own thoughts, doubts, fears, or feelings—all of which we must acknowledge in order to cut to our essential spiritual core. In fact, developing faith requires an honest and heartfelt search for answers to meaningful doubts. This view was aptly summarized in Emerson's belief that honest doubt contained more faith than most creeds found in religion. (see Ralph Waldo Emerson, *Essays* [Boston: Houghton Mifflin & Co., 1865]).

Faith requires us to study, ponder, pray, and seek understanding from our own efforts and experience, both temporal and spiritual. Certainly doubts must be overcome to gain the spiritual power that resides in faith, but faith itself does not mean being solely compliant or having an accepting state of mind. Neither does faith mean avoiding the difficult and searching questions that naturally spring from a desire to learn. And most of all, faith is not a form of mind control we can exercise in an attempt to minimize the influence of some of our thoughts and feelings that are not in harmony with God's will.

Faith is engaging in that experiment described by Alma (Alma 32:27) in which we awaken and arouse our faculties to apply personally the teachings of the Savior. All experiments begin with questioning, with a desire to inquire and search out truth. Then with questions in mind, even with a doubting mind, we put to the test the promises made in the scriptures that if we seek, we shall find. Such spiritual experimentation must be attended by an acknowledgment of our weaknesses, a critical element that cannot be ignored if the experiment is to be successful.

Faith begets faith. It is strengthened by our own experimentation with principles of righteousness. As the value of each principle is tested, refined, and confirmed by our own experiences with it, our faith gradually becomes stronger, which in turn strengthens our spiritual identity. We, through experience, are then more inclined to define ourselves in spiritual terms, which increases our willingness to behave like spiritual beings, which bolsters our identity even more.

Some may mistakenly assume that introspection, listening to ourselves, and relying on what we hear is a sign not of faith but of willfulness and perhaps even rebelliousness. In fact, the contrary is true. If we are righteously self-governing, we always place the principle first, never ourselves. In so doing, both the principle and the individual are served. Putting the principle first requires a teachable attitude, a willingness to be open and honest with ourselves and others, and an acceptance of responsibility for our own thoughts, feelings, and behaviors. That openness places us in a very vulnerable position, one in which others have greater opportunity to know us as we really are, thus increasing the likelihood of our being accepted or rejected. Is it not an act of faith to be so open to judgment and criticism? Righteous self-government is risk based on faith, faith in our spiritual self and faith in the Lord regardless of what others think.

A change of heart. As our faith in the Lord and our ability to discern right from wrong increase, a change takes place within us. That fundamental and enduring change is essential to authentic spirituality. Alma the Younger recorded: "Did not my father Alma believe in the words which were delivered by the mouth of Abinadi? And was he not a holy prophet? Did he not speak the words of God, and my father Alma believe them?

"And according to his faith there was a mighty change wrought in his heart. Behold I say unto you that this is all true.

"And behold, he preached the word unto your fathers, and a mighty change was also wrought in their hearts, and they humbled themselves and put their trust in the true and living God. And behold, they were faithful until the end; therefore they were saved.

"And now behold, I ask of you, my brethren of the church, have ye spiritually been born of God? Have ye received his image in your countenances? Have ye experienced this mighty change in your hearts?" (Alma 5:11–14).

This change of heart is the initial influence of our spiritual identity taking a more assertive place in our lives. It is not unlike repentance. The fourth article of faith tells us that repentance follows faith in the Lord Jesus Christ. According to Elder James E. Talmage, repentance "embodies (1) a conviction of guilt; (2) a desire to be relieved from the hurtful effects of sin; and (3) an earnest determination to forsake sin and to accomplish good. Repentance is a result of contrition of soul, which springs from a deep sense of humility, and this in turn is dependent upon the exercise of an abiding faith in God" (*The Articles of Faith* [Salt Lake City: The Church of Jesus Christ of Latter-day Saints, 1982], 109).

With an "abiding faith in God," we submit ourselves to a standard of accountability higher than our own. The contrition and humility that follow compel us to confess and forsake those things that we and the Lord find unacceptable. That demonstration of faith increases our personal worthiness, which makes us more sensitive to our spiritual identity, which then increases our intolerance for those times when we heed external voices rather than our own internal sense of right and wrong. Repentance follows, and the cycle begins again. Faith and repentance intertwine and complement each other in this refining process. But this is not merely one massive step, and we have arrived. We must repent continually and, in the process, attend ever more closely to our spiritual identity, which is the fundamental receptor of the influence of the Holy Ghost. Exercising our spiritual identity causes it to grow stronger and stronger.

Charity. In 1 Corinthians 13:1–4 we read the Apostle Paul's stirring description of charity: "Though I speak with the tongues of men and of angels, and have not charity, I am become as sounding brass, or a tinkling cymbal. . . .

"And though I bestow all my goods to feed the poor, and though I give my body to be burned, and have not charity, it profiteth me nothing.

"Charity suffereth long, and is kind; charity envieth not; charity vaunteth not itself, is not puffed up."

After we have begun to develop faith and we experience a change of heart, the next step is to make our behavior truly an extension of who we are inside. Charity is the link that connects motives to behavior and allows our spiritual identity to be made known to others. The Book of Mormon defines charity as "the pure love of Christ, and it endureth forever; and whoso is found possessed of it at the last day, it shall be well with him" (Moroni 7:47). Christlike love compels us to alleviate the suffering of others when we are aware of it. If a brother or sister is going without, charity impels us to feel compassion and then do something about it.

Charity is both what we do to help others and the underlying motive or feeling for doing it. Charity is crucial to our spiritual identity because it is the means whereby we can physically manifest that identity. We cannot grow or progress alone. Without others, we are unable to prove our worthiness by the way we act toward them. Without those who could benefit from our charity-motivated help, our spiritual identity would remain static and nonfunctioning. With charity, we can "assist in this work" (D&C 12:8), which is all the good works our Father wants us to be engaged in during mortality. The following story illustrates how faith, change of heart, and charity combine to cultivate spiritual identity.

Calvin grew up in a lower-middle-class family. Things were always scarce, and generosity from others was not one of the hallmarks of his childhood. It was quite natural, then, that he learned to fight for everything that he got and to share nothing for fear that there would never be enough. Consequently, he grew up to be quite selfish and defensive.

Later he joined the Church. He was a bright young man, and the fundamental meaning and purpose of such crucial Christian concepts as charity, service, and compassion were not lost on him. Yet he knew he was not the least bit charitable, compassionate, or interested in serving others. His life had been too cold and hard for those qualities to have been instilled in him.

Calvin could have participated in any number of Church activities that would have made him appear much more charitable than he really felt. But he had read the scriptures carefully and was fully aware of the significance of charitable motives and compassionate intent. He saw little point in simply trying to pretend to be better than he knew he was.

He didn't know exactly what to do, but he knew something very deep inside him would have to change before any charitable acts he performed would be congruent with what he felt. Out of sheer desperation, he took his problem to the Lord. The intensity of his prayers was powered by fundamental discontent with a part of himself, as well as a growing concern that he would never be able to overcome such a basic defect in himself. So, he prayed in earnest, he prayed with humility, and he prayed because he understood that nothing else would really help him.

Eventually, Calvin was touched by the Spirit of the Lord. He felt that he had been forgiven of his sins, though he had no explanation for that belief. He just knew the feeling was new, different, and as powerful as it was peaceful. But he felt more than that. He experienced what he had never experienced before—the Lord's love for him. He learned what charity was by being treated charitably. He would never be the same again, inside or out. His internal deficit was gone. He cherished the way he had been treated by the Lord, and it seemed entirely natural to him to treat others in a similar way—not because he was supposed to, but because he wanted to.

He could have chosen to minimize his internal conflict

about being selfish rather than openly acknowledge and face his feelings. Had he done so, however, he would have failed to make the preparations necessary for the Lord to make his redeeming power known in such an intimate way. Clearly, then, Calvin's willingness to recognize his problem for exactly what it was may well have been the first step he could take in overcoming it. But the deeper sense of charity he acquired was not entirely the result of his own efforts. It was a gift. And the gift was given by God in the way Calvin could most easily understand. When he experienced the Lord's benevolence, he also experienced a small part of his own capacity for godliness. He was so touched and moved by the kindness and generosity of deity that his heart was softened and changed. The result of that change was that Calvin now wanted to serve others because of his own enriched sense of spiritual identity.

We live in a society that continually invites us to betray the guiding influence that emanates from our internal/eternal identity by emphasizing such external values as superficial appearances, wealth, status, achievement, and power. Enhancing our identity involves paying attention to our own thoughts and feelings and responding to them instead of to socially mediated ones. This process enhances our effectiveness, however, only when we own up to our deepest thoughts and feelings without denying or distorting them. Enhancing our identity involves a process that is not just the result of hard work or one hundred percent attendance at meetings. It is the result of humbly acknowledging our weaknesses and directly experiencing the Lord's benevolent care and regard for us. Our individual experiences with deity create charitable hearts and enhance our awareness of our spiritual identity. Those experiences are gifts given in grace as we attempt to overcome our weaknesses. Once we experience the Lord's charity toward us, it is natural for us to extend to others the warmth and regard we have received from him.

The essential spiritual and psychological processes involved in the development of our internal/eternal identity primarily involve ourselves and the Lord. The development of our identity is enhanced by an attitude of daily repentance rather than self-aggrandizement because that is the only attitude that allows us to learn from our spiritual and psychological weaknesses.

Once we begin to develop our spiritual sense of who we are, the requirement of righteous self-government that we do the right things for the right reasons becomes infinitely easier to meet. With faith in the Lord and faith in ourselves, we face adversity and opposition knowing that regardless of the outcome, we can approve of ourselves and be approved of by the Lord. With a change of heart, we become more receptive to the promptings of the Spirit through our spiritual self when temptation beckons and the lines between right and wrong blur. With charity, we become the conduit through which Christ's love is manifested through our love for others. Being becomes doing. We become righteously self-governed in thoughts, feelings, and actions.

....

CHAPTER FIVE

WE CAN'T GIVE WHAT WE HAVEN'T GOT

AN ANCIENT POET WROTE, "There are many that pass for holy men who keep foulness in their hearts and go through the external ablutions of saints in order to hide their sins" (*Kural, the Great Book of Tiru-Valluvar,* trans. C. Rajagopalachari [Bombay: Bharatiya Vidya Bhavan, 1965], 48). Such people were typified by the scribes and Pharisees of the New Testament and the lawyers in the Book of Mormon (Mark 7:5–6; Alma 10:17). They outwardly professed righteousness, but their motives were not pure. There was little harmony between who they represented themselves to be and who they really were. They lacked congruence, which is the degree to which people's actions reflect what they truly think and feel.

SELF-INVENTORY OF PERSONAL CONGRUENCE

Congruence is another word for harmony between how you act on the outside and what you think and feel on the inside. The more congruent you are, the more harmony there is between the inner and the outer you. The following exercise will help you measure your own congruence:

SCALE

  1 = This statement is true of me MOST of the time.
  2 = This statement is true of me MUCH of the time.

3 = This statement is true of me SOME of the time.

4 = This statement is true of me ALMOST NONE of the time.

Questions

_____ 1. I stay in unsatisfactory relationships just to avoid being lonely.

_____ 2. I laugh at jokes even though I don't think they are funny.

_____ 3. It is easy for me to express my opinion of my boss to my co-workers without ever telling my boss what I think of him or her.

_____ 4. I avoid discussing certain subjects with people who are close to me in order to avoid hurting their feelings.

_____ 5. Although I willingly help others, it is very difficult for me to let others know I need their help.

_____ 6. I am extremely sensitive to criticism regardless of how accurate it is.

_____ 7. It just isn't worth the hassle of having the waiter take my order back when it is not prepared the way I requested.

_____ 8. After I've argued with someone, I spend quite a bit of time thinking about what I wish I had said but didn't.

_____ 9. I have my current job more out of financial necessity than interest or career planning.

_____ 10. If church attendance weren't a commandment, I'd go to my meetings less frequently.

Your score may be as low as ten or as high as forty. The higher the score, the more likely you are to have a clear sense of spiritual and psychological congruence.

WHAT IS CONGRUENCE?

Congruence, the second leg of our three-legged stool of righteous self-government, is the unification of what we are on the inside with what we appear to be on the outside. Ideally, it means that our actions are in harmony with our internal/eternal identity.

Congruence is a powerful part of our human effectiveness. It is the way our identity fully expresses what we really feel and think and, therefore, what we really are. We must be aware, however, that the road to congruence is filled with such dead-ends and chuckholes as anger, selfishness, impatience, and greed. These are as much a part of our human nature as virtuous qualities. So, how are we to deal congruently with those less-attractive qualities and impulses as well?

Again, the answer involves the process of self-evaluation in light of our internal/eternal identity. When we evaluate ourselves, not only do we recognize and respond to our true thoughts and feelings but we also respond to the thoughts and feelings we have about our original thoughts and feelings. The following story will help explain this important concept.

Tim feels angry. His anger and resentment are understandable, considering what others did to him. He wants to get even. If he were to act congruently with his feelings, he would show his anger and get even. Congruence requires it. But if we add self-evaluation to this story, we get an entirely different outcome. Tim must now look at his thoughts and feelings and decide what he thinks and feels about them. As we said, his anger and resentment are understandable, considering what others did to him, and he wants to get even. But there is far more to Tim than just the anger and resentment. So he asks himself not only what he is thinking and feeling but also how he feels about what he is thinking and feeling. Does he approve? Does he disapprove? Is he happy with himself? Is he disappointed in himself?

Self-evaluation in light of our internal/eternal identity is no minor addition to our description of congruence. It changes the whole standard of being congruent. Because self-evaluation is completely independent of the original event and the feelings it created, it adds a new dimension. Tim can now feel the anger and resentment that was already there, but in addition he must acknowledge and accommodate the feelings of self-approval or disapproval created by his own self-evaluation.

Being congruent requires far more than merely expressing our first thoughts and feelings; it involves being congruent with our own deeper self-evaluation as well. We simply cannot act in ways we disapprove of and still be congruent. When we are congruent, we evaluate our thoughts and feelings based on our inherent sense of right and wrong and then act accordingly. The prophet Nephi exemplified this concept in prayer, in which he evaluated his own thoughts and feelings:

"And why should I yield to sin, because of my flesh? Yea, why should I give way to temptations, that the evil one have place in my heart to destroy my peace and afflict my soul? Why am I angry because of mine enemy?

"Awake, my soul! No longer droop in sin. Rejoice, O my heart, and give place no more for the enemy of my soul.

"Do not anger again because of mine enemies. Do not

slacken my strength because of mine afflictions" (2 Nephi 4:27–29).

Nephi was angry with his enemies. Yet, instead of acting out this anger, he examined how he felt about being angry, and he was not pleased. Based on his self-evaluation, he vowed no longer to "droop in sin" but to elevate his thoughts and feelings from anger to a desire to trust the Lord in all things.

Congruence is a skill. It is acquired and strengthened over time by consciously being honest with self and others. It involves the risk of first knowing ourselves and then allowing ourselves to be truly known by others. It adds to our spiritual and psychological strength, but only after we face and acknowledge our weaknesses.

Psychologist Carl Rogers referred to honest self-expression as being unafraid to present ourselves as we really are. There is no need to be defensive, to deny deficiencies, or to hide mistakes. All of us at one time or another are ignorant when we should be knowledgeable, prejudiced when we should be open-minded. If we can come out wearing no defensive armor, making no effort to be something other than who we really are, we can learn more, get closer to people, and ultimately enjoy life much more (see *Freedom to Learn,* 2d ed. [New York: Merrill, 1985]).

CONGRUENT WITH THE TRUTH

Being congruent with the truth is central to our theology. President Harold B. Lee summarized spiritual congruence as true conversion, evidenced by our outward behavior reflecting an internal acceptance of eternal truth: "One is converted when he sees with his eyes what he ought to see; when he hears with his ears what he ought to hear; and when he understands with his heart what he ought to understand. And what he ought to see, hear, and understand is truth—eternal truth—and then practice it. That is conversion" (*Stand Ye in Holy Places* [Salt Lake City: Deseret Book, 1974], 92).

The apostle James definitively explained the importance of knowing and then acting congruently with eternal truth: "But be ye doers of the word, and not hearers only, deceiving your own selves.

"For if any be a hearer of the word, and not a doer, he is like unto a man beholding his natural face in a glass:

"For he beholdeth himself, and goeth his way, and straightway forgetteth what manner of man he was.

"But whoso looketh into the perfect law of liberty, and continueth therein, he being not a forgetful hearer, but a doer of the work, this man shall be blessed in his deed" (James 1:22–25).

CONGRUENCE AND CONFORMITY

It is sometimes easy to confuse personal congruence with giving in to feelings of guilt or self-consciousness, a misplaced sense of duty, or any other unhealthy perception of how we think we are supposed to act. This unfortunate tendency is not even remotely related to the congruence that leads to a durable sense of self-approval. For example, a friend has been sick for several days. We are busy and haven't yet found the time to visit him. We think we should, but things keep coming up. After a long day at work, we finally arrive home hungry and tired. Suddenly, we remember that we still haven't visited our friend. After a short debate with ourselves, we drag ourselves out of the house and back into the car to go visit our friend. Our motive is a sense of guilt mixed with duty, not interest and affection. We go mostly because we think we should. After the visit, we are glad we went, but we are also relieved that we have satisfied our sense of duty to a friend and won't have to worry about it any more.

This situation is one in which acting without congruence might be considered the right thing to do. It is, after all, only a small act of incongruence, one that appears to benefit someone in need. It is very common to find situations like this in which a small act of incongruence takes the form of doing something good but for the wrong reason. What is the problem with handling such a situation without congruence? Consider the following points:

1. The visit was motivated by guilt and a sense of duty more than compassion or a sincere desire to be helpful. Such motives usually remain well concealed during any such visit. Imagine going home teaching or visiting teaching when we really don't want to. Now imagine letting the family or sister know that we really don't want to be there. How would we feel if someone visited us and let us know the visit was made simply to report 100 percent home teaching or visiting teaching? Once the motive for the visit is made plain, the value of the visit disappears. Therefore, the alleged value of the visit can be maintained only by deception. Generally speaking, then, whenever we are unwilling to publicly own up to the motives behind our behavior, we can be certain that the quality of our behavior is questionable, no matter how desirable it may appear.

2. Few people would even want a visit motivated by guilt and obligation rather than personal interest and concern. Furthermore, no one responds favorably to being deceived or being the object of a required service project.

3. Finally, and most importantly, we do great damage to ourselves when we are incongruent. The damage may not be immediately obvious, but it is still present and powerful. It is analogous to the cancer cell that can't be seen. As long as it goes undetected, it can spread malignancy so quietly that its deadly power is hardly noticeable until it is too late.

The spiritual and psychological cancer of incongruity is dangerous to the development of our internal/eternal self. For example, when we lack truly charitable motives but behave in ways that appear to be charitable, we excuse ourselves from the important task of facing and overcoming our lack of charity. Even little acts of incongruence conceal parts of ourselves that need improvement. In our example of visiting a sick friend, the most important issue is not whether we make the visit. Rather, it is examining why we don't want to go in the first place. Facing that issue would bring us face to face with the spiritual cancer cells in our own character. Grudgingly visiting the sick without self-evaluation only masks the selfishness that lurks inside.

Congruence combined with humility increases our awareness of personal weaknesses, which is the first step in improving ourselves. Furthermore, such congruence is essential in developing positive regard for self and others. The following story illustrates these points.

The divorce was final. No more yelling. No more pleading. No more wondering when he was going to leave again. But Sharon had no idea that with the sense of relief would come a new kind of pain—that of an empty house, a cold bed, and meals eaten alone.

Still, she refused to believe that all hope was entirely gone. Miracles do happen. But when Brad remarried just seventeen days after the divorce, all hope ceased. The world fell in on her. There was no place to hide the horrible, ugly truth. Her temple marriage had failed. She had failed. Everything that had ever mattered was in ruins. And so was she. Why should she even bother getting out of bed in the mornings?

At first she tried to be big about it. Of course, it was all a lie, but she tried anyhow. That's just the way she was. She sent a gift to Brad and his new wife, wishing them well. She went to work to provide for herself. At night she lay in bed and cried. She made it a point not to complain, particularly when her children were home. She wanted to be a forgiving Christian in the face of real adversity. To others, she appeared strong and forgiving, but to herself she was a pathetic failure. Eventually, the burden of maintaining a solid front to hide her broken heart became more than she could bear. As her depression worsened, family, friends, and church leaders finally convinced her to seek professional help.

At first it was difficult for Sharon to talk as openly as she needed to. But the more she did, the better she felt. Her therapist noticed, however, that she seemed to be avoiding many of her most intense feelings. Given her extreme circumstances, her hurt, anger, and disappointment seemed perfectly natural to him. So he kept asking her why she wanted to hide her most important feelings from herself and from others.

No matter how many different times and ways he asked the question, she always seemed stunned by it. He finally asked her to identify all the feelings that she wanted to conceal because they seemed inappropriate and unchristian. The implications of that question greatly upset her. But it was an important question, and she knew it. She thought about it all week.

Her next session was one she will not easily forget. Sharon

walked in, sat down, and without the slightest hesitation began talking. She was in charge. She spoke precisely and with conviction. Her therapist was amazed at the transformation. Sharon was no longer a helpless victim, though she didn't seem to be aware of it herself.

"I have taken a good look at myself this week, and I don't like what I have seen," was the first thing she said. She then reported in exquisite detail everything about herself she had so meticulously tried to avoid the week before. She had found the courage to look inward and acknowledge her real thoughts and feelings, and now she had the resolve to deal with them. She was being congruent at a time when it was the most difficult for her to be so.

She didn't wish Brad and his new wife well—she deeply resented them both. Brad had had no business abandoning her. She was angry. She was hurt because of the divorce. But her most negative feelings had nothing to do with him. She was mostly upset with herself. Why? Because she wanted to do everything in her power to see that Brad would not be happy in his second marriage. She wanted him to fail. Acknowledging that about herself hurt deeply, but it felt good to say it because it was the truth.

As they talked, Sharon became aware of two inescapable facts. First, she had faced the truth about herself and her feelings. She didn't like what she saw, but she liked her willingness to face the truth. That felt hopeful and reassuring to her. Second, although a part of her felt angry, petty, and vindictive, another part of her did not approve of those hostile feelings. Therein lay the value of her self-evaluation: she was able to recognize her negative feelings, which then allowed her to disapprove of them.

In trying to overcome her anger and vindictiveness, she no longer presented herself as long-suffering and charitable. Rather, she acted as she truly was: someone who was trying to become long-suffering and charitable and in the process was asking the Lord, her family, and ecclesiastical leaders to assist her along the way. Her behavior was now congruent with what she truly thought and felt.

OBSTACLES TO CONGRUENCE

If being congruent is so desirable, why is it so difficult? Think about it for a moment. As children, we probably all had the experience of being chastised or reprimanded for telling the truth about our feelings. Back then, that behavior was probably called being rude or disrespectful. Similarly, as adults we may have noticed that we can stop a good group discussion by simply expressing our deeply held views on what is being discussed. Personal relevance or intensity just seems to make others uncomfortable.

Our difficulty in being congruent results from our simply having become accustomed to its opposite. For instance, how often have we told someone we liked their sacrament meeting talk when we really didn't—or didn't even listen—or said our feelings were not hurt when they were, or greeted someone with a handshake and a smile while having ill feelings toward that person. We all do it to one degree or another. Ironically, our attempts to fool everyone rarely fool anyone. Everyone understands the game of incongruence: look good, fit in, and don't rock the boat. In exchange, we will act as if we like and accept each other at face value, but we will still harbor disbelief, skepticism, and maybe even some resentment.

As incongruence for the sake of acceptance and social

comfort increases, personal credibility decreases. It is a strange trap to be caught in. The more we convey agreement with others when it differs from what we actually feel, the more we compromise the quality of our own character. Usually we call it being supportive or tactful, but we hardly ever call it what it is: fear of being ourselves.

We all have our own good reasons for being incongruent. It could be something as simple as shyness or as crippling as shame. Incongruence is a way of controlling our feeling self-conscious and minimizing the risk of rejection by being what others want us to be. But such psychological elasticity can be dangerous. At one point or another we may become confused about which is the real us and which is the one we present to others for their approval.

Enhancing Personal Congruence

Increasing our capacity for personal congruence and honest self-evaluation involves taking the risk of knowing ourselves, of being known by others, and of behaving intentionally.

Knowing Ourselves

Truly knowing ourselves means increasing our awareness of our primary thoughts and feelings, particularly those that may be unpleasant or frightening. Accurately understanding ourselves can be risky because it creates the possibility of finding out that our greatest fears might be true—for example, we really are selfish, unlovable, lazy, mean, and so on. Though it does not always feel good to know the truth about ourselves, it always feels good to know that we are willing to face that truth. The following case study illustrates how this principle works.

Clint was in therapy because of deeply conflicting feelings about his father. He was twenty-six, married, and without children. He had reported many favorable experiences with his father. All of them seemed to show his father as being genuinely concerned with his family's well-being: he was a good provider but one who valued family more than professional opportunity and who was always available to help when needed.

In this particular session, Clint spoke of his conflicting feelings about spending Labor Day weekend on a family picnic his father had arranged rather than getting away with his wife for two days. It was clear this young man preferred to go away with his wife but felt that would be disloyal to his family in general and his father in particular.

After carefully listening, the therapist said, "You seem to have difficulty accepting your feelings of resentment toward your father for smothering you." Clint recoiled. The comment was obviously on target. The therapist then asked Clint to close his eyes for five minutes, turn inward, and, without saying anything, try to identify his feelings toward his father at that moment. Finally, Clint opened his eyes and announced, "I really do resent him. I didn't realize how much." Though he found those feelings unacceptable, they were now his. He then was able to explore openly what it was about himself that made it so difficult to become emancipated from his somewhat overbearing father. The idea of resenting his father still does not sit well with Clint, but he makes no attempt to deny the reality of it to himself.

BEING KNOWN BY OTHERS

Learning to know ourselves involves acquiring knowledge about ourselves, but being known involves letting others know who we really are—what we value, think, and believe. This process is both natural and reasonable, but it usually feels difficult and uncomfortable. The biggest problem with making ourselves known is that when we openly declare who we are, we also open ourselves to criticism and rejection by those who may not share our views and values. Nevertheless, making ourselves truly known to others does have its unique rewards: it is the basis for building authentic and enduring relationships, feeling genuinely understood by others, and strengthening our personal integrity. The following story illustrates these rewards.

At the end of two days of interviews, the candidate for employment met with the president and his two vice-presidents for lunch. During the meal, the president indicated that they all had been favorably impressed and wanted to offer him a position. The candidate replied that he appreciated the thoughtful and courteous way he had been treated during the visit, but he felt he must decline the offer. Puzzled, the chief officials pressed him for the reasons for his refusal. The candidate asked how honest they wanted him to be in clarifying his reservations. They insisted on absolute candor.

For the next six hours, they discussed the company's deficits in professional integrity, work habits, and simple honesty. The candidate stated that he would find it personally embarrassing to be affiliated with the company irrespective of salary or prestige. The company officials appreciated his candid views so much that they offered him a consultantship to focus exclusively on developing integrity in the organization.

Their offer was undoubtedly the result of the candidate's presenting himself in a way that truly reflected his own views and values. The administrators could just as easily have been insulted and thrown him out. Regardless of the outcome, however, the candidate would have left with his personal integrity intact because he had acted congruently with his internal/eternal identity.

BEHAVING INTENTIONALLY

By nature, we humans seem inclined to prefer the known over the unknown and comfort over discomfort. That inclination can hinder personal growth because trying something new almost always involves the unknown and thus discomfort.

Learning to be congruent is certainly no exception. Because there is discomfort involved, the choice to increase personal congruence is almost always the result of a deeply felt desire to become more honest with ourselves and others. Unless we have that desire, it is just about impossible to increase our congruence, particularly when society values simple appearances as much as or more than behavior that is an expression of our real character. This is why intentional behavior is necessary to foster congruence. Behaving intentionally is a deliberate expression of our choice to become different. We choose to improve ourselves, and we know where to start because we acknowledge our weaknesses. Behaving intentionally not only leads to increased congruence but is itself an act of congruence.

PERSONAL DEVELOPMENT EXERCISE

The following exercise can help you enhance your personal congruence:

On a sheet of paper, list three situations in which you feel you have been incongruent, situations in which you spoke or acted differently from the way you really think or feel.

Next, list the words that most accurately describe how

you think and feel about yourself for having behaved incongruently.

Now, imagine that you have the chance to relive those three situations. Write down how you would behave if you were to act with congruence.

List the words that most accurately describe how you would think and feel about yourself when you have behaved congruently in those situations.

Share with someone important to you the results of this exercise. Discuss with that person the steps you would like to take to improve your congruence.

Congruence is synonymous with righteous self-government. When we do the right thing for the right reason, our behavior matches our motives—what we do is simply a reflection of what we are. Consider, for example, a person with religious doubts and little faith. He may wish it were not so, but the fact of the matter is, he's a chronic doubter. He could pray for assurance. He could act as if he believed more than he really does. Many might even commend him for those approaches, saying that such actions will increase faith. But congruence asks more of us. It requires us to openly acknowledge our limited faith to ourselves first and then to our Heavenly Father in candid prayer. It requires us to say on bended knees, "Lord, I am a person of limited faith. Please 'help thou my unbelief.' Bless me that I may come to know thee."

Ironically, many of us fail to realize that openly facing our weaknesses and deepest concerns creates the humility that makes us most receptive to divine assistance. Congruence means acknowledging all of our weaknesses squarely as a way of becoming strong. And when it comes to dealing with other people, congruence means refraining from putting up fronts or roadblocks and acting in ways that are congruent with our best self, our internal/eternal self, and thus having nothing to hide. This level of congruence builds relationships and character.

With congruence between our actions and our internal/eternal self comes a strength that influences all facets of our lives. Because pretense no longer exists, energies that we once spent on maintaining facades and fooling others can now be directed toward more efficacious activities. We experience a sense of relief when we openly acknowledge fears that we have kept hidden from ourselves and others. In that moment of honesty, congruence abounds.

ON OUR OWN BUT NEVER ALONE

A BASIC TASK OF ADULTHOOD IS TO be truly self-directing, to achieve a healthy emotional and psychological independence that allows us to find the balance between the unique factors that differentiate us from others and the common characteristics that we share with them. If we simply choose to echo those around us, we have little chance of making a meaningful contribution. Being self-directing requires us to be more than just a reflection of those around us. Thoughts, feelings, and behaviors should converge to create a person who is free and willing to be righteously self-governing. Mortality is the time and the place to learn how to live independently according to principles that lead to enduring spiritual well-being. That is autonomy.

SELF-INVENTORY OF PERSONAL AUTONOMY

Autonomy means our ability to independently follow our righteous thoughts and feelings. The following exercise will help you measure your personal autonomy:

SCALE

> 1 = This statement is true of me MOST of the time.
> 2 = This statement is true of me MUCH of the time.
> 3 = This statement is true of me SOME of the time.
> 4 = This statement is true of me ALMOST NONE of the time.

QUESTIONS

____ 1. At one time or another I have questioned my beliefs to determine whether they are truly my own.

____ 2. I arrange for time alone, so I can reflect on the way my life is going.

____ 3. When I am alone, I seldom have trouble knowing what to do with myself or my time.

____ 4. I allow those I love to know me as I truly am.

____ 5. I share my thoughts and feelings with others as they occur.

____ 6. I am open to taking some emotional risks with those I love the most.

____ 7. I know when to trust my own judgment and when to rely on the counsel of others.

____ 8. I am willing to take responsibility for my own decisions, even when they are wrong.

____ 9. I am as much a leader as a follower in my circle of family and friends.

____ 10. I am willing to ask questions of those in authority over me when I do not understand or agree with what they say.

Your score may be as high as forty or as low as ten. The lower your score, the more likely you have a clear sense of autonomy.

SPIRITUAL AUTONOMY

If we describe identity as the storehouse for our values and attitudes, and congruence as the bridge that joins our identities to our behavior, then autonomy is the sense of independence necessary to cross that bridge. The scriptures leave no doubt about the important role of autonomy in our spiritual development. A very dramatic illustration is found in Moses:

"And I, the Lord God, commanded the man, saying: Of every tree of the garden thou mayest freely eat,

"But of the tree of the knowledge of good and evil, thou shalt not eat of it, nevertheless, *thou mayest choose for thyself,* for it is given unto thee; but, remember that I forbid it, for in the day thou eatest thereof thou shalt surely die" (Moses 3:16–17; emphasis added).

Choice, agency, and accountability—the key ingredients of autonomy—are paramount in this dialogue between God and Adam and Eve. The Lord clearly advised and instructed but then added, "Thou mayest choose for thyself, for it is given unto thee." The important role of agency in the face of opposition could not be illustrated any more clearly nor at a more crucial time.

The degree to which the views and values of the parent (God) were openly declared but not imposed is also important. Even though God clearly acknowledged and reminded his children of their agency, he did not remain neutral or even vague about what constituted appropriate and inappropriate conduct. Also, notice the clarity and directness of his language and instructions: "Of every tree of the garden thou mayest freely eat, but of the tree of the knowledge of good and evil, thou shalt not eat of it . . . ; remember that I forbid it."

There is no ambiguity or uncertainty here. God is exhorting, persuading, and instructing, but he is making no attempt to control. God was as clear and emphatic in reminding his children of their agency to disregard him as he was in expressing his own views and values. What an intriguing application this passage of scripture could have in our dealing with our own children: exhort, persuade, instruct, but don't control.

Autonomy is the final basic ingredient of righteous self-government. The following story illustrates what autonomy is and how it influences our lives.

It was a warm summer evening. The mountain breezes were pleasant and seemed to hold the promise of erasing the gnawing tensions of a long and unpleasant day. The bishop was not eager to start his evening interviews with ward members. He was tired. No, he was worn out. Just appearing interested in the problems he was about to face was going to be difficult. But he would try. What else could he do? He decided to take some lawn chairs to the most private corner of the backyard. He would have the evening interviews in the cool night air. Maybe that would help. He also prayed silently for spiritual strength and guidance for those he would try to serve.

He looked at his schedule. The first two appointments were minor matters. The third was a temple recommend interview, and the fourth was a marital problem. After that it would be time for the problem he had dreaded all day: Dale and Lori.

Eventually the time came. Dale and Lori sat down and started talking. Lori was the kind of person who needed to spend at least an hour a week with her bishop. Life had not been good to her. Although she was young, she knew a lot about loneliness, rejection, and sorrow. She worked hard at being a good Christian, partly because it was the only thing she truly trusted and partly as a way of desperately clinging to a source of help with personal problems that could overpower her at times. She and Dale had recently started dating. Even though his family was active, he had not been interested in religion since he was about eighteen, and he didn't see any need to pretend that he was. His honesty and candor spoke well of him.

They were meeting with the bishop at Lori's insistence. During the last two weeks their good-night kisses had become petting. Lori found herself completely unable to stop the advances of somebody who seemed to really care for her. She was desperately hoping the bishop could help them.

They talked a long time. It gradually became clear to the bishop that years of unmet needs for attention and affection were pushing Lori into activities she didn't approve of but couldn't resist. It was equally obvious that Dale was not spiritually grounded and simply did not have any abiding reasons to refrain from expressing himself sexually.

As they talked, the bishop gradually became aware of a growing feeling most bishops experience from time to time. The Comforter was present. The bishop discerned it was for Dale's benefit, so he asked Dale if he could feel it. Dale was confused by the question. Eventually he said no. The bishop asked Dale to pause and turn inward and see if he could notice a feeling he may have never noticed or felt before. Dale paused a long time before he said yes. The bishop explained the meaning and origin of the subtle but poignant feelings that were present and their significance in this conversation. For the first time in his life, Dale was exposed to the spiritual source for valuing personal morality. It was not overwhelming, but it was real. It was a beginning.

When the conversation ended, the bishop offered to meet with Dale the next week, if he wished. The bishop emphasized that spiritual development required constant work. He also told Dale that the spiritual feelings he had experienced this evening were not common, and similar experiences in the future would require much more of him. It was clear that Dale had some important choices to make.

Dale had been introduced to the still, small voice of the Spirit, and his experience was sufficient to cause him to pause, reflect, and investigate—if he wanted to. And he now had reason to want to. The meaning of the moment spoke for itself. It may not have been a loud, ringing voice, but it was clear and distinct from all others. He had been carefully taught a small but important lesson of the Spirit.

Personal choice, agency, and accountability were now operative in Dale's life. His future depended entirely on what choices he made in light of his new but limited knowledge. That knowledge had been given without coercion, manipulation, condition, or expectation. It could be cultivated or disregarded, pondered or forgotten. But because this experience was his alone, it was equally clear that no one else was responsible for what he did with it.

Psychological Autonomy

The closest psychological relative of spiritual autonomy is *locus of control*. The similarity between this important psychological term and its theological counterpart is considerable: they both deal with issues of choice, self-direction, and motive.

Locus of control refers to the degree to which individuals believe that their choices and actions influence what happens to them. Those with an internal locus of control believe that their choices and actions matter. These people tend to believe that wise choices and hard work are much more important to success than such external considerations as luck or fate. Those with a more external locus of control perceive many events to be beyond their influence or control. These people are more inclined to view themselves as helpless victims of outside, arbitrary forces and capricious circumstances.

Quite naturally, then, individuals with an external locus of control generally shrink from important life choices because they believe that their efforts make little difference. A good illustration of this point of view can be found in the way many individuals passively accept such hard economic realities as inflation, unemployment, and corrupt business practices.

Individuals with an internal locus of control respond to situations much differently. These people believe that their decisions and actions matter. They gather information before making decisions and consider alternatives before acting. They are not inclined to see themselves as passive victims of the world that surrounds them. They choose what they will allow to affect them, they decide what goals they will pursue and when, and they accept more responsibility for what happens to them. So when problems arise, they seek information and create alternatives that allow them to make important choices about how they will respond to difficulties in their lives.

The ability of such individuals—"internals"—to influence what happens to them is illustrated in James Fenimore Cooper's novel *The Deerslayer.* At one point in the story, a prisoner (who has an internal locus of control) is brutally tortured by Indians. Yet, by controlling his mind, he never lets his would-be assassins see his fear. Although physically restrained by being strapped to a tree, he still has control of the situation. The baffled Indians stop their abuse, and the prisoner obtains his freedom.

Though this example may appear dramatic, the underlying pattern that differentiates "internals" from "externals" is always the same: internals believe that what they do makes a difference, and because they believe their choices and efforts make a difference, they do more to direct their own lives. Externals believe that what others do makes the difference, and so they wait to see what will happen to them.

Decades of research are showing that internals and externals have qualitatively different life experiences. And the scope of these differences is sweeping, including such diverse considerations as mental health, physical health, education and income, political activity, and personal values. And the emerging pattern is equally clear. Internals tend to be happier, healthier, and more productive, and they live with less stress.

CHARACTERISTICS OF INTERNALS AND EXTERNALS

Mental Health

Internals	Externals
Optimistic	Pessimistic
High morale	Low morale
Copes with conflict	Avoids conflict
Persists in completing tasks	Prematurely ceases efforts
Is a leader	Is a follower
Is usually happy	Is usually depressed
Is calm	Is anxious
Seeks intrinsic rewards	Seeks extrinsic rewards
Is creative and alert	Is inattentive and blindly traditional
Values choices	Is burdened by choices

Physical Health

Internals	Externals
Values preventive care	Values medical advice

Accident free	Accident prone
Is healthier	Is less healthy
Recovers rapidly	Recovers slowly
Values self-care	Values expert care

Social Considerations

Internals	*Externals*
Plans for future	Lives day-to-day
Is socially involved	Is socially isolated
Persuades others	Attempts to coerce others
Is proactive	Is reactive
Uses little stereotyping	Tends to use stereotypes

Education

Internals	*Externals*
Earns higher grades	Earns lower grades
Goal oriented	Needs outside direction
Is creative in thinking	Is rigid in thinking
Self-motivated	Motivated by approval

Individuals who are more adept at exercising their God-given right to personal autonomy, individual choice, and agency experience life quite differently from their less fortunate and more easily controlled counterparts. Individuals who have taken it upon themselves to "choose for thyself," as instructed by the Lord in the Garden of Eden, seem to prosper for their efforts.

At first glance, a high level of autonomy could appear spiritually dangerous, particularly when obedience to spiritual authority is also important to our salvation. That concern quickly fades, however, when we realize that God granted us agency to aid our spiritual and personal development. Choice and agency work only in our favor when we exercise them with righteous intent—when we do the right things for the right reasons. When we understand more completely God's values and principles and what he expects of us, it is clear that without autonomy, obedience is nothing more than compliance in the absence of choice, a state that completely precludes spiritual or personal development. The following story illustrates how and why individual autonomy enhances our spiritual and psychological development.

Steve didn't know if he wanted to go to college, so he asked his dad what he thought. But his father wanted to know what Steve thought. So Steve told him. He was worried about failing, he was worried about money, he was worried about stress, but he was also worried about the consequences of not going to college.

Steve wanted reassurance. Steve's father wanted him to make an independent decision. So they talked. Yes, money would be a serious problem. The family would help as they could, but Steve would have to invest heavily and consistently in his own future. Yes, failing was a real possibility. Though Steve was a capable student, he was not the best. Yes, stress could become a big problem. Competition would be keen, and success was not assured. And yes, the consequences of not going to college were significant: less income, less fulfilling employment, and fewer opportunities. After reviewing and clarifying the facts, Steve wanted to know what his dad thought, but his dad still wanted to know what Steve thought. So they talked some more.

Eventually Steve decided. His reasoning went like this: "I am going to college, but I understand it is a big risk and sacrifice for me. I will have to really get it together and keep it together if I am going to succeed; however, not going to college exposes me to even bigger risks, over which I can have no control. I think I can make it if I work hard, and I would think more of myself for trying."

So Steve went to college, worked hard, and graduated. He was a good student, though not the best. Other students with more "brains" and more money failed, but he succeeded. Why? Because he decided to go, because he paid the bills, and because he decided to face the difficulties. When he came face-to-face with these difficulties, Steve felt responsible for handling them, and he did. And his father was very proud.

The old adage "He who gathers his own firewood is twice warmed" explains what Steve experienced. Because Steve made his own decisions and paid for his own education, success in school was more meaningful to him. But the importance of this concept extends well beyond self-satisfaction. Exercising autonomy creates the condition for maintaining or enhancing intrinsic motivation. Choosing his own path provided the very impulses for him to succeed.

This point is lost on parents who insist on subsidizing every activity for their children and then wonder why nothing comes of it. At the other end of the spectrum, parents who dictate, demand, and demean will have little luck in sustaining their children's compliant behavior when they are not there to enforce their parental will. In the absence of choice, the absence of motivation is sure to follow. The converse is equally true: with choice, motivation flourishes.

ENHANCING AUTONOMY

Autonomy and internal self-direction are crucial to effective living. We can always expect to find ourselves in situations where doing the right thing is not the popular thing. But for the authentic internal, such a situation is an opportunity to show their thoughtfulness, their fairness of mind, and their resolve to live by principles. Enhancing autonomy requires us first to look at a factor that stifles it: shame. "Like a wound made from the inside by an unseen hand, shame disrupts the natural functioning of the self.

"Because shame is central to the conscience, indignity, identity, and disturbances in self-functioning, [shame] is the source of low self-esteem, poor self-concept or body image, self-doubt and insecurity, and diminished self-confidence. Shame is . . . the source of feelings of inferiority. The inner experience of shame is like a sickness within the self, a sickness of the soul. If we are to understand and eventually heal what ails the self, then we must begin with shame" (Gershen Kaufman, *The Psychology of Shame* [New York: Springer, 1989], 5).

As long as we harbor unrealistic shame and the resulting self-doubts, the chances of our achieving autonomous thinking and behavior are remote. The fear of being shamed often prevents us from acting on our own feelings and perceptions. This response creates in us a reliance on others to tell us what to do to gain approval and acceptance. And as long as that disturbed dependence exists, achieving autonomy is next to impossible.

Shame is restricting. It stops us from venturing out of psychological comfort zones and taking the risks necessary to develop independence, which comes from exercising the unique qualities each of us has. In many respects we then become psychologically isolated, harboring past moments of shame and embarrassment like little secrets that, if discovered by others, will only contribute to our ever-mounting sense of shame. The secrets can be large or small, recent or as old as our first memory.

The important point is whether we perceive our shameful moments as something we feel or as something we are.

A healthy sense of shame can contribute to our understanding of our own imperfection, help us cultivate a healthy conscience, and motivate us to improve ourselves. On the other hand, if we become overwhelmed with shame, we think of ourselves as flawed or defective. This type of shame has deep, strong roots, and it usually requires professional assistance to overcome. When our identity becomes excessively influenced by shame, doubts interfere with our ability to assert our own opinions. We are unable to act from our personal convictions, because we are unwilling to risk them by sharing them with others. Ultimately, this inability stops us from behaving in ways that are congruent with our inner self—and that is paramount in developing autonomy.

Steps for overcoming shame suggested by many prominent psychologists include the following:

1. *Acknowledging the shame inside ourselves.* As with all troublesome things, we must recognize that a problem exists before we can resolve it. That is particularly important in the case of shame. Shame-based people are unable to acknowledge just how bad they really feel. Their shame is tucked away in places they prefer to forget exist. But refusing to consciously acknowledge shame does not stop it from influencing their lives. The shame simply manifests itself in less obvious ways: failure in relationships, depression, anxiety, a lack of direction. People who suffer from toxic shame can only rid themselves of it by first admitting that it exists. Acknowledging shame is described by John Bradshaw in his book *Healing the Shame That Binds You* (Deerfield Beach, Fla.: Health Communications, 1988). He lists several steps, five of which are mentioned here:

a. Honestly share feelings with significant others.

b. Talk about what we feel shames us. Write in our journals or diaries about past events that make us feel ashamed now.

c. Learn to recognize when we talk negatively about ourselves to ourselves. There are negative and positive "voices" in our heads. The negative voices sabotage success and predict nothing but failure. Stop them by questioning the truth of what they are saying. Are we always failures? If we make one mistake, does that mean we are completely bad?

d. Learn how to handle mistakes, and have the courage to be imperfect. Shame can drive us to try to be perfect, something we cannot be on our own. Consequently, when we do make mistakes, shame causes us to degrade ourselves even further.

e. Learn through prayer and meditation to create an inner place of silence wherein we ground ourselves in what we would call our internal/eternal selves.

2. *Finding a higher power.* For a person to be whole, the spiritual aspects of individuals must be attended to and, when difficulties arise, called upon for help. We are, after all, spiritual beings having a human experience. Finding a higher power means recognizing that our shame may be greater than we can handle and, after all we can do, seeking strength from the Lord to help us overcome our shame and find ourselves worthy of his love and the love of others. By relying on the Lord, we go beyond our own situation or experience to surpass what we are capable of doing on our own.

3. *Sharing secrets and risking depending on others.* Shame compels us to keep secrets about our private selves that we believe would shame us if we openly admitted them to ourselves or

divulged them to anyone else. That is regrettable for at least three very important reasons.

First, if we do not risk knowing ourselves as we truly are, we harbor weaknesses that can never become strengths because we ignore them in the hope that they never existed in the first place or that by some magical process they will eventually go away. Holding on to our weaknesses, of course, deters us from growing, sharing ourselves fully with others, and striving to emulate the Savior.

Second, keeping secrets locked away inside of us causes them to become the filters through which much of our behavior and perceptions are processed. Things appear worse than they really are. New experiences become tainted with old shame. Eventually, even the most positive things are distorted, minimized, and dismissed. That process is incredibly effective in stopping our progress. Who can find the energy or a reason to change when everything appears so bleak?

Finally, keeping secrets allows the negative aspects of ourselves that are true to grow way out of proportion. Bad things become horrible things as they thrive on our silence. And because there is no way to test our secrets against a more objective standard that sharing with others provides, we find it increasingly difficult to discern just exactly what is real about us and what isn't. In extreme cases, our minds fabricate negative images about ourselves that have no basis in reality at all.

Until we allow others to share our burden and extend to us a compassionate hand, shame can eat at us until we feel totally consumed by it. We must depend on one another when our own ability is lacking. There is no shame in that, only the risk of increasing shame if we don't.

4. *Differentiating between healthy and toxic shame.* Healthy

shame is essential if we are to monitor and then correct ourselves. Healthy shame is synonymous with conscience. Such
feelings of shame, remorse, and self-disapproval motivate us to
repent, change, and grow. Healthy shame, then, is essential to
our psychological and spiritual development. But when shame
becomes toxic, it does exactly the opposite. It motivates us to
distort, deny, and hide things about ourselves from ourselves,
others, and the Lord. It is crucial to know the difference
between these two types of shame: one moves us to do better;
the other keeps us from getting better.

If past events in our lives have contributed to our sense of
shame now, it may be worthwhile to seek the help of our families, friends, and ecclesiastical leaders and to obtain professional counseling, if necessary. We should not underestimate
the power of shame. It binds and limits us, for it decreases
autonomy and deters us from being self-directed.

FREEDOM

As doubt and shame dissipate, the heaviness of depression
that accompanies toxic shame lifts. We feel ourselves free from
the bonds of perceived past failures. We see more options for
thoughts, feelings, and behaviors. Where once our automatic
response to threatening and shame-inducing situations was to
run, withdraw, and numb out, we now recognize our fear and
then exercise our ability to choose an appropriate response.
This freedom is a function of our internal/eternal selves, not of
our circumstances or surroundings.

In the absence of debilitating shame and doubt, freedom
increases. Exercising that freedom produces psychological har-
diness and strength: the ability to influence others, determine
our own direction, and retain our sense of identity when social

influence and pressure threaten to swallow it up in a sea of conformity. Our psychological hands are no longer tied. We are free to pursue areas that show promise for growth and positive development. Such strength allows us to learn from others, gleaning from them whatever is uplifting without sacrificing our own sense of self. It allows us to follow a worthy leader without being deterred from our own life course and opportunities to lead. It enables us to acknowledge our own weaknesses and mistakes without defensiveness and with a desire to do better. In other words, such strength promotes our autonomy.

Operating from strength means we can be ourselves and allow others to be themselves. Strength provides a degree of composure that those who are weak cannot have. Feeling constantly threatened, they remain defensive and ever on guard. Afraid of not having their own needs met, they perceive life as a win-lose proposition. "I can only win if you lose" is their mentality. They deal with others in an emotionally hoarding way because they think, "The only way I can get what I want is if you do not get what you want."

On the other hand, psychologically strong individuals perceive life as a win-win arrangement. They understand that helping others meet their needs will actually help them meet their own needs. Service to others becomes spontaneous and genuine.

Autonomy is epitomized by charity without compulsion. We do not wait to be asked to serve. We serve independently and with gratitude for the opportunity. The more acts of kindness we perform, contributing to the strength of others, the stronger we become.

Mark was a young high priest who had been assigned to home teach a retired couple in the ward, the Durrants. Sister

Durrant had been bedridden for three years. Her husband had cared for her with a devotion and love that were undeniable. But as time passed, Brother Durrant's health began to fail. Slowly, almost imperceptibly to their neighbors, things worsened for the Durrants. But apart from a yard that could have used a good weeding, there was little anyone could see that truly reflected the problems this couple was having.

After two or three months of perfunctory visits to the Durrants, Mark began noticing signs that this couple's life was not running smoothly. Brother Durrant wore the same shirt regardless of its stains. A few letters scattered here and there had turned into piles of unopened correspondence. Mark avoided staying long because of the musty, sickly smell that the Durrants' home had acquired.

When Mark returned from his last visit to the Durrants, he shut off the engine of his car and just sat in the driveway. A vague but undeniable discomfort overcame him. He felt just plain overwhelmed. Things were a mess on all levels of the Durrants' lives: they needed help with finances, help with upkeep on the house, personal hygiene, meals, not to mention their need for visitors and friends and things to keep them occupied.

Mark's mind raced. He didn't want to be bothered by someone else's problems. He liked the Durrants, but he didn't like them enough to get so intimately involved in their lives. Shouldn't their family take care of them first? Why should he have to take the responsibility that the Durrants' children were evidently not taking? He felt like calling the high priest group leader and asking for a change of assignment. Give the Durrants to another home teacher who was closer in age, had the same interests, lived closer to them, could spend more time with them. Mark found himself compiling a fairly impressive list of reasons why he shouldn't home teach the Durrants anymore. And with each excuse, they sounded more and more like just that—excuses.

The discomfort he felt got worse as it became clear to him that he was really feeling guilt and shame. He had recognized right from the first moment he stepped into their house that things were not going well. But he remained appropriately detached and fulfilled his home teaching in a timely, albeit superficial, manner. And now, more than ever, Mark didn't want to go back. The discomfort of being overwhelmed by a potentially large task had grown into the searing pain of self-realization: recognizing, understanding, and acknowledging his unchristian feelings when what was needed more than anything else was a willingness to be Christlike.

In one excruciating moment, Mark was faced with a monumental decision: would he run from his own disapproval and allow shame to dictate how he would behave toward the Durrants, or would he do what was necessary to feel good about himself and what he understood on a very fundamental level to be worthy of his priesthood? Closing his eyes, he uttered a silent prayer. He didn't ask for inspiration. He didn't need it. Things were painfully clear. He didn't ask for strength to face a difficult duty. He still wasn't willing to face it. He didn't ask for help at all. He asked for forgiveness—forgiveness for thoughts and feelings that were selfish, forgiveness for trying to justify his selfishness. He then asked for a softening of his heart so that his compassion for the Durrants would exceed his natural aversion to helping them.

Mark first demonstrated his autonomy by recognizing the true source of his discomfort as he sat in the car and thought over the Durrants' situation. He was ashamed of himself for trying to justify his desire to avoid behaving charitably. He was sufficiently self-aware to understand how he was trying to fool himself, and he was psychologically strong enough to acknowledge his rationalizations and call them what they were. He then went one step further and evaluated his thoughts and feelings. He didn't like what he came up with. He then openly acknowledged to the Lord what he had experienced and prayed for forgiveness. That was the essential first step in forgiving himself and setting aside the shame that could compel him to simply remove himself from a difficult situation.

The entire process up to this point was done privately, internally, autonomously. Furthermore, Mark recognized his own weakness—that of not feeling sufficiently charitable toward the Durrants—and sought the Lord on that count before he could go any further. This he had to do alone. No one could do it for him.

Mark could have maintained his superficial relationship with the Durrants. He could still have reported 100 percent home teaching, and no one would have been the wiser. By forcing the issue in his own heart and mind, without the intervention of an ecclesiastical leader, a request from the Durrants themselves, or any other external influence, Mark acted autonomously. In addition, he knew that what he was capable of giving toward the solution of the problem that evening was simply a commitment to be more prayerful. He autonomously and honestly assessed his abilities and acted on them, not beyond them. Many shame-based individuals try to respond as something either more or less than what they truly are. Mark, on the other hand, was accurate in assessing what he could give, and he acted upon that ability.

Mark's service to the Durrants waxed and waned again and again. With every new crisis, Mark had to decide just exactly how he was going to respond. His autonomy was by no means a static state that, once achieved, never faltered. On the contrary, it was a process that constantly demanded attention and cultivation. It was no small task some months for Mark to make more than the required single visit, which he knew would be enough to satisfy external demands. Few people really knew the extent of the Durrants' needs or of Mark's help to them, and so there was little praise. To maintain the level of commitment needed to help the aging couple required an ability to behave in ways that were independent of praise and recognition.

Cultivating autonomy is a fundamental task of mortality. The degree to which we are able to express ourselves congruently determines just how independent we are of the desire to simply please and placate others. Furthermore, autonomy is closely related to locus of control: do we feel that what we do matters? Are we in control of our own lives, or do we give up that control to external factors, reducing ourselves to the role of victim? Autonomy means we understand who we are, and are willing to risk being ourselves regardless of circumstance. That requires us to look at ourselves in a way that we alone are capable of. Do we like what we see? Are we ashamed? Is the shame warranted, or does it extend to past experiences that must be acknowledged and reckoned with before we can be free of our own disapproval and the unrighteous disapproval of others?

Spiritual autonomy goes well beyond psychological well-being. It requires much more of us. Spiritual autonomy demands that we abandon the temporary, imperfect ego and recognize our divine origins. Through our ability to discern between our spiritual selves and our psychological selves, we are able to love God first, which frees us to love our fellow beings. Autonomy can be frightening because we risk doing away with what is familiar and under our control in order to allow the Spirit to direct us. Spiritual autonomy is the ultimate level of personal responsibility: to be worthy to receive inspiration directly from the Lord and then have the courage to act upon it righteously. In that sense, autonomy is an active, vibrant process. President Spencer W. Kimball described the need for righteous activity this way: "People tend often to measure their righteousness by the absence of wrong acts in their lives, as if passivity were the end of being. But God has created 'things to act and things to be acted upon' (2 Nephi 2:14), and man is in the former category. He does not fill the measure of his creation unless he *acts,* and that in righteousness. 'Therefore to him that knoweth to do good, and doeth it not,' warns James, 'to him it is sin' (James 4:17).

"To be passive is deadening; to stop doing is to die" (*The Teachings of Spencer W. Kimball,* ed. Edward L. Kimball [Salt Lake City: Bookcraft, 1982], 148).

CHAPTER SEVEN

STOPPING SELF-DECEPTION

SOME INDIVIDUALS SINCERELY BELIEVE they are completely innocent in moments of conflict and that the other person is to blame. These are not shallow convictions that are subject to change with discussion and reason. They genuinely trust their own perceptions, and what they usually perceive is that conflict is someone else's fault, not theirs.

No one is excused from this most human tendency. We all do it to one degree or another. The truth of the matter is that most of us are quite adept at seeing the fault in others while remaining comfortably oblivious to our own. C. S. Lewis describes this lack of self-understanding as a classic tool of the devil to keep us from "discovering any of those facts about [ourselves] which are perfectly clear to anyone who has ever lived in the same house with [us] or worked in the same office" (*The Screwtape Letters* [New York: Macmillan, 1982], 16).

The scriptures teach us that our ability to see our own faults is crucial to our own progression and to the progression of those with whom we associate as well. In Luke we read: "And why beholdest thou the mote that is in thy brother's eye, but perceivest not the beam that is in thine own eye? Either how canst thou say to thy brother, Brother, let me pull out the mote that is in thine eye, when thou thyself beholdest not the beam that is in thine own eye? Thou hypocrite, cast out first the beam out of thine own eye, and then shalt thou see clearly to pull out the mote that is in thy brother's eye" (Luke 6:41–42).

This scripture is often used in discussions about hypocrisy to make the point that we must not criticize others because none of us is free of shortcomings. Nevertheless, these verses do not command us to refrain from pointing out their weaknesses to others. That is part of the responsibility we have to contribute to the growth of our brothers and sisters. Rather, these verses make the important point that we can remove the mote from their eyes only if we have removed the beam from our own eye first. As with the Savior's admonition in Luke 22, "When thou art converted, strengthen thy brethren" (v. 32), our priority in dealing with imperfection is to help ourselves and then to help those around us.

The implications of this concept are compelling. At the bottom of most inadequate human behavior is the capacity to see things in ways that are inaccurate and self-serving even if they are ultimately self-defeating. This problem is made worse by the fact that even in the very midst of distorting things, many of us truly believe that we are not deceiving ourselves at all. That happens most often when we stand to benefit in some way, particularly if that benefit is excusing us for our own faults.

Psychological beams are as small as blaming traffic for your habit of being late for appointments or as large as being abusive to family members because "that's how I was raised." The process can be seen in the recovering alcoholic who minimizes the hazard of taking a route home that will lead him past the bar he used to frequent or in the person struggling with a weight problem as he attempts to downplay the harm of a second dessert. In both cases, however, such small details are usually the first steps in a sequence of events that leads to serious and potentially dangerous behavior. When it comes to our own vulnerabilities, there is no such thing as a small or insignificant decision.

Other beams are larger and more long-standing. They may cause great discomfort to us and distort the way we see things. But because they have been with us so long, it is difficult for us to name them or recognize how deceiving they can be. These beams can be self-made or made with the help of others. They can be as wide as the fundamental way you view yourself and the world or as slim as a little quirk that shows up only on specific occasions. Regardless of a beam's shape or size, it can stop us from doing the right things for the right reasons or even from doing the right things at all.

THE ESSENTIALS OF SELF-DECEPTION

When we are sick and go to the doctor, we report our symptoms, the doctor asks a few questions and orders a blood test, an X-ray, or some other diagnostic procedure. Then he says, "This should tell us what's really going on in here." He can make such a statement because of his training in normal and abnormal biological functions. When he finds out what's wrong, he usually knows what can be done to fix it. All of what he does is based on the assumption that when abnormal processes are identified and corrected, normal health will be restored.

With respect to spiritual and psychological health, things are a bit more complicated. What constitutes normal development is never as obvious, and what can be done to fix abnormal development varies greatly from one individual to another. Despite the complexities, however, some types of problems are readily recognizable, as are their effects. Two common beams that interfere with our seeing clearly are irrational thinking and life scripts. We may possess these beams with varying degrees of awareness. They stop us from facing what is embarrassing, frightening, or otherwise upsetting. This in turn produces motives that are designed to keep us away from such discomfort. And as long as we avoid discomfort, we lose opportunity to grow. We must be willing to question ourselves, and evaluate our perceptions. Until we do, we will never know what beams are there.

IRRATIONAL THINKING

As young children, we learned to accept what others told us as being accurate interpretations of reality. How and what we felt about ourselves was largely contingent upon the feedback of others. Such feedback usually came from our parents, but the influence of teachers, friends, and other people at school and church all contributed to our ultimate views about life and our place in it. That is all very natural when we are young, but as we grow older, the irrational nature of many such beliefs can cause trouble. Most of our feelings of depression, anxiety, and rejection can be the result of beliefs that originate in childhood and remain essentially unexamined in adulthood.

Dr. Albert Ellis proposes that the way we think about life events determines how we feel about them (see *Humanistic Psychotherapy: Rational/Emotive Applications* [New York: Julian Press, 1973]). This beam appears as faulty and irrational thinking, which creates negative self-evaluations and emotional distress. That is a fairly radical idea for those who tend to attribute their unhappiness to bad circumstances and uncontrollable events, something that could have been learned very early. The alternative is that life events in themselves do not create our unhappiness but that the irrational way we think about these events is the real cause of our unhappiness. For instance, Sister Jackson has spent the past month preparing her Spiritual Living lesson for Relief Society. She gives an excellent lesson, but few sisters give her a positive response. Sister Jackson is disappointed and saddened, wondering what she did wrong. She even begins to question her ability to teach. The more she thinks about it, the worse she feels.

Three basic components are involved in Sister Jackson's distress. The first is the reception she received from the Relief Society. The second is Sister Jackson's beliefs about what happened, including such negative thoughts about herself as "I did something wrong" and "I shouldn't teach another lesson." Third is the emotions she felt: hurt, loss of self-confidence, and sadness.

It may appear that the reception Sister Jackson received is the cause of her distress. On the other hand, it could be her beliefs about what happened (the beam of irrational thinking) that are the real cause of her problem. If we could read what is engraved on her irrational beam, we would likely see such sentences as "It's my fault that nobody liked my lesson. I should have prepared more and made my visual aids just a bit nicer. I'm a really inadequate teacher. What a disaster!"

Sister Jackson's thinking is saturated with self-criticism. Anyone who thinks this way would be upset, but such self-punitive thoughts are unwarranted and irrational. Those negative thoughts have caused Sister Jackson's distress, not the fact that she didn't receive the compliments she had hoped for.

If Sister Jackson had learned to recognize her beam of irrational thinking, she would have been able to remove it with more rational ways of looking at things. Examples of clearer thinking might include, "It hurt when no one commented on how well the lesson went. I wonder what was different in the way I gave this lesson compared to others I have given. I'm sorry that very few sisters seemed inspired by what I said. Oh well, I did my best. I can't expect rave reviews every time I teach."

There are three primary kinds of irrational thinking:

1. I must win the approval of important people, or I am an inadequate person.

2. Others must treat me fairly and considerately all the time.

3. My life must be easy and pleasant.

Many of us automatically resort to two powerful irrational thoughts when any of our life assumptions are not satisfied. First, "This is horrible." Second, "There must be something wrong with me." Whose feelings would not be profoundly influenced by such irrational and self-punitive thoughts as these? Learning to examine carefully and then replace our own irrational thoughts with more rational ones is an important first step in reducing the needless frustration of unwarranted negative self-evaluations.

The beam of irrational thinking can stop us from doing the right things for the right reasons and being righteously self-governed. As long as we are prone to think negatively of ourselves or catastrophize even small disappointments, we will avoid engaging in activities that could cause us to feel bad. In Sister Jackson's case, she was considering giving up teaching. A closer look shows that her intense preparation was not to present a lesson that would contribute to the knowledge and testimonies of her sisters but rather to avoid something she greatly feared: failing to receive praise. As long as she was blinded by the beam of irrational thinking, she would continue to do the right thing for the wrong reason.

SELF-EVALUATION EXERCISE

1. What types of events or situations upset you the most? List three of them.

2. When you are actually in these situations and you are upset, what do you say to yourself about yourself and the event that upsets you the most? Write three sentences you say just the way you say them to yourself at the time.

3. Answer the following questions in the way that reflects how you usually behave: Do you tend to see unpleasant events as catastrophies? Do you recognize any irrational elements in your thinking? Do you challenge your irrational thoughts and replace them with more realistic ones? List three typical events in which your irrational thoughts most likely appear.

4. Finally, list three rational thoughts that you can use to replace the irrational thoughts that you identified in question 2.

LIFE SCRIPTS

Just as a movie or a play unfolds according to its script, so, in large measure, do our lives. Regrettably, many of us may not be fully aware of the script our lives are following. More importantly, our life script may not be the one we would consciously choose.

Life scripts are made up of the beliefs and assumptions we have accepted about ourselves, usually as youngsters—beliefs and assumptions we may not even remember acquiring. Some common life scripts include being a loner because we have been taught that others can't be trusted; being dominant and aggressive because we have been taught that to be otherwise is a sign of weakness; being underachieving and mediocre because we have been taught that others will resent our success.

Our life script can become the core of our identity. It may consist of such unfavorable assumptions as "I am an unlovable person" or "I will never succeed at anything." It can also be made up of such favorable and positive assumptions as "I can count on myself to do the right thing in difficult situations" or "My personal feelings are a good guide for successful living." Life scripts continue to influence our feelings and behavior long after we have forgotten how or when we learned them, as is the case in the following story.

Henry started making provisions for his approaching retirement and eventual death. Throughout his entire life he had been a loner. To many he seemed unreasonable and demanding, with little capacity for insight or change. He worked hard to provide for his family but was not particularly appreciated because of his unpleasant personality. He frequently fought with those he loved, felt lonely and hurt most of the time, and seriously doubted that anyone could really love him. As he thought about his remaining years, his first concern was to provide for his wife. He had always loved her and tried to gain her approval by taking good care of her. That was all he felt he had to offer. It had never really worked, however. There had been a few good months now and then, but on the whole, the marriage was filled with conflict and hostility.

Henry's instructions to his family were quite revealing. He was to be placed in a "home where old men go to die" once he became too much trouble for his children to take care of. Money from his estate was to be set aside to cover expenses for himself and his wife, and the remaining money was to be divided among the children equally. He said more than once that "people could visit me if they wanted," but he didn't expect them to. When his wishes were discussed, the family objected to his "poor me story," just as they always did, and expressed their affection and desire to take care of him. Of course, Henry disregarded their tender comments.

This is the true story of a man who was preparing to die in exactly the same way he had lived. He attended to the needs of others as a way of gaining their approval and then acted like a martyr, so alienating others that they hardly knew how to respond to him. Then he would feel lonely, hurt, and uncared for, even though he cared for others.

The underlying theme of Henry's life script is fairly obvious: the world is cold and uncaring, and a good man must suffer while serving those he loves. Henry had learned this unhealthy script as a child in a home that was essentially cold and uncaring. Henry created all the necessary emotional deprivation so he could suffer throughout his adult life just as he had as a child.

Such illustrations are sad, but the consistency of some peoples' self-defeating behavior across their entire lives is most easily understood as a reflection of their life scripts. Henry's script called for him to suffer, so he did; but his suffering was pointless. He neither understood nor abandoned the life role he had adopted, not even in preparing to die.

Negative life scripts create the most distorting kinds of beams because they have been with us for so long. To understand how life scripts can become so powerful, we need to understand the messages we receive, beginning early in life, that tell us what we are, what we are good for, how the world works, and what our place is in it. These messages can be conveyed in a variety of ways, some subtle and some obvious, such as the way we are treated, how often we are ignored, how and when we get love, and how and when we get punishment. We start receiving these messages, usually from our parents, at such an early age that we accept them as absolutely true. It is not unusual for us never to fully recognize or examine them. They can simply become the organizing basis of our personalities, directing what we think and feel. Robert and Mary Goulding identify what they consider the most common messages taught to children and how they affect their development (see *Changing Lives through Redecision Therapy* [New York: Grove Press, 1979]):

1. *Don't.* Children who continually hear and accept the message "Don't . . . " gradually come to believe that they cannot do anything right. As a consequence, they often look to others to make their decisions for them.

2. *Don't be* is a terribly destructive message usually conveyed indirectly by parents who wish their children hadn't been born. Those who have received such a message may well spend their entire lives working endlessly to get others to love them.

3. *Don't be close.* Two other messages are closely tied to "Don't be close." They are "Don't trust" and "Don't love." Those who have been affected by any of these messages may avoid intimacy and meaningful relationships as a way of not being hurt again.

4. *Don't be important.* There are many different ways the message "Don't be important" can be received, but one of the most powerful is to be regularly ignored. It isn't surprising to find that children who receive this message grow up thinking of themselves as unimportant. Such people minimize their

successes and keep a low profile as a way of being true to their life script of being essentially unimportant people.

5. *Don't be a child.* The core of the message "Don't be a child" is "Don't have fun," "Always stay in control of yourself," and "Always act like an adult." The result is that individuals who believe this message may avoid letting themselves have a good time because it may appear childish or immature.

6. *Don't grow.* Parents who are frightened about the prospects of their children growing up, becoming independent, and eventually leaving them often convey the message "Don't grow." It is not unusual for children in these families to try to maintain their parents' approval by staying in the role of a child long after it is appropriate.

7. *Don't succeed.* When a child is reinforced for failing (that is, parents offer protective consolation after failures rather than encouraging personal responsibility), children may accept that as a message to refrain from seeking success. The most typical response to this message is a willingness first to accept and then to expect failure.

8. *Don't be you.* The message "Don't be you" is most commonly received by a child whose parents wanted a child of the opposite sex. Such a message requires the child to try to be more like the opposite sex as a way of gaining parental approval.

9. *Don't be sane.* Tragically, some children get attention only when they are in trouble, physically sick, or acting crazy. These children come to believe that the only way to get attention is to have something wrong with them.

10. *Don't belong.* When children don't fit into the family, they may come to believe they won't belong anywhere. The natural result is often to become loners throughout life.

Such messages may run throughout our lives. Naturally, it can be difficult to be aware of just how destructive some messages are if they are all we have ever experienced. It can be equally difficult to unlearn them and replace them with new and more constructive ones, but it is important to become aware of the silent forces that often direct our lives without our permission. The following questions may help us do that.

SELF-EVALUATION EXERCISE

1. What three powerful messages have you accepted that influence the way you think, feel, and act?

2. What are some of the messages you have received concerning your self-worth? your intelligence? trusting others? your ability to be loved? your capacity to give love?

3. Who was most influential in shaping the way you see yourself: your mother, father, grandparent, or friend?

4. Write down the important messages you accepted from this person.

Some of us may find it helpful to consciously rewrite our life scripts to give ourselves a new pattern to follow. Patriarchal blessings may serve a similar purpose in changing the direction of our lives.

Mortality often provides the circumstances for us to acquire beams. Some may be deeply embedded psychological flaws; others, nagging spiritual imperfections. Regardless of their origin, however, they impair our ability to do the right things for the right reasons. They manifest themselves to us in challenges with pride, a lack of charity, or vanity, or, as the following story illustrates, they can be totally imperceptible until their effects are felt profoundly.

If appearances counted for anything, Mike had to be solid

gold. Good-looking, athletic, and infectiously enthusiastic, he exuded confidence and class. He had tailor-made suits and a wife and three children that fit him just as well. Mike was the sort of guy that you automatically gravitated to at church or at neighborhood functions. It was a gift, his ability to make you feel comfortable and accepted even if you'd known him for only five minutes.

And Mike's friendliness went beyond mere social pleasantries. Having been called as the Sunday School teacher for the fifteen- and sixteen-year-olds, it was obvious from his well-prepared lessons and the extra time he spent with his students that he was conscientious and ever willing to go the extra mile. Whether at church or in the community, you could count on Mike to be there when help was needed.

Within a year's time, the ward Young Men president was transferred by his company, and no one was surprised when Mike was called to replace him. Mike was a natural with the youth in the ward. He tackled his new calling with the same energy and drive that attended everything he did. Not even the most recalcitrant youths could stay away from the activities he organized. He offered jobs to three priests who were notorious for being irresponsible troublemakers. His small manufacturing business was an ideal spot for the young men to work a couple of hours after school cleaning up and doing odd jobs.

Mike had become someone you could trust. If he didn't volunteer first, you could bet that he would accept an assignment and carry through with it. Temple excursions, ward dinners, Explorer campouts, youth conferences—Mike was there. So when Mike approached the bishop about investing in his business, there was little hesitation. Other ward members also heard Mike's investment proposition, which seemed well conceived and involved only minimal risk. His neighbors were interested in investing with someone as reliable and competent as Mike.

Six months later, the bishop, ward members, and neighbors were horrified when Mike's business was closed by the Securities Exchange Commission. Mike was eventually found guilty of fraud and sentenced to five years in prison.

We could easily dismiss this as a story of a wolf in sheep's clothing—a person who looked like a good guy but was really a deceitful con man. The truth is, Mike's intentions were never malicious, and he was certainly not interested in consciously hurting people who trusted and respected him.

Mike worked hard and accomplished much, but if we were to get inside his head for a moment, we would see that Mike's good works were a product of his need for acceptance and approval. He met the needs of others only as a way to meet his own needs. In the process, he rationalized his dishonesty by reminding himself of all the good things he did. That is the point where behavior and motive diverge, where the difference between righteous self-government and unrighteous facsimiles becomes apparent. Because righteous and unrighteous behavior can appear identical, it behooves us to continually evaluate our own actions and determine the goodness of our intent. Mike never did. He found that the more he volunteered, said yes, and gave to others, the more credible his internal argument became that if he did good things, he was a good person, despite his dishonest business dealings. His motives for doing good works became an effective way of denying his dishonest actions.

Mike was completely aware that his business was failing. How could he ask for the money of good, trusting people, knowing there was little chance that they would get their money back, let alone any kind of profit? Beams. Spiritual and psychological flaws allowed him to deny the gravity of his situation, to deny that his actions were deceitful and illegal. He had learned through his life that approval depended on pleasing others. His life script dictated that he present a positive front, even if it was false, because if he showed anything that even appeared negative, others would reject him. The beam in his eye was inscribed "People require what looks good." As long as they didn't know the bad things that were going on, everything would be all right. He went to his business every day and worked hard. At church on Sunday he took the sacrament. The beam in his eye grew so large that it blinded him from even thinking of the dishonesty of his behavior. In fact, he prayed for strength to work harder.

"It's not stealing," he thought. "They're investing in me. I can make things work. Besides, I've done a lot for this community. They can keep me floating until I get my feet back on the ground, and then I'll pay them back." Such thinking gave his conscience just enough room to slink away. And as long as he remained unaware of the beam in his eye, he continued his behavior until he was caught.

Irrational thinking and life scripts typically occur without our conscious choice, but we expend large amounts of energy in using them, energy that could be used for far more constructive thoughts and behaviors. When we spend our effort to cover up our weaknesses, we sap our own spiritual and psychological strength. Each time we avoid facing our weaknesses, we have less and less energy to face them. And as long as we remain blind to the beams in our own eyes, we have little chance of doing the right things for the right reasons.

....

CHAPTER EIGHT

MAKING WEAK THINGS BECOME STRONG

ONE GREAT CHALLENGE OF RIGHTEOUS self-government is to acknowledge our failings instead of ignoring them. Acknowledging weakness is the first step in the process of making weak things become strong. In the October 1951 general conference, Spencer W. Kimball, then a member of the Quorum of the Twelve, said, "I believe it was from this very pulpit that my grandfather presented a sermon in which he said, 'The test, the *test*, the TEST is coming.' Well, the test is here. The test has always been here. We came into the world as a test. All the way down the line there are adjustments to make. There are sins to overcome. There is much to learn. There are weaknesses above which we must rise. We must gain self-mastery, become righteous, and attain *unto* perfection" (in Conference Report, Oct. 1951, 84; emphasis in original).

A critical activity of our mortal existence is to make adjustments, overcome sins, learn much, and rise above our weaknesses—all of which leads to self-mastery, righteousness, and, ultimately, perfection. In fact, there would be no righteousness in the absence of our having weaknesses and sins to overcome. That principle was made evident in Lehi's admonition to Jacob: "It must needs be, that there is an opposition in all things" (2 Nephi 2:11). But because of our natural tendency to look upon our personal weaknesses with disdain, we instinctively want to hide them—from ourselves, from others, and from our Heavenly Father. What a remarkable blueprint we have followed since our first earthly mother and father hid themselves from the Lord because they realized they were naked. The only way Adam and Eve could reestablish their relationship with God was to confess their wrongdoings and suffer the consequence of their disobedience by being expelled from the garden. But that is only the first part. The second and more important part is that a world that groans under sin and darkness (see D&C 84:49) now provided the environment in which their mortal weaknesses could be manifested and overcome so that they could ultimately return to the Father.

Imperfection always precedes perfection. We can't skip imperfection—it is a necessary part of mortality. If we ignore that fact, we risk keeping our weaknesses, doubts, and nagging bad habits hidden. Not only does hiding our weaknesses stop us from overcoming them but usually makes them worse.

Kurt was unpretentious and easygoing. In his midthirties, he had a wife and four children. They were a family that anyone would have liked to have live next door. Friendly, well-mannered, and always willing to help, they appeared to be living a typical middle-class life. Kurt often got backaches so severe that they interfered with work. But his wife still baked cookies and took them to the widow across the street, Kurt still coached the priests' basketball team, and when the home teachers came over, everything appeared just fine.

Kurt went from doctor to doctor trying to find the cause of his debilitating pain. Each doctor gave him a new prescription for pain; each prescription was for something stronger and more habit forming. When one pill didn't work, Kurt would take a second and then a third. His wife would gingerly ask him if he was taking too much. In his usual quiet manner, Kurt would tell her that everything was okay.

As time went by, Kurt's latest doctor grew reluctant to write more prescriptions for him. He wanted to admit him to a pain hospital where they could control his treatment, but Kurt said he could handle things on his own. The doctor said he couldn't keep giving Kurt prescriptions without new tests and a possible hospital stay. Kurt refused, even though he was now missing two or three days of work a week, but whenever his mother called to see how the family was doing, he said everything was just fine.

Then his last prescription ran out three weeks before it should have because he was taking three times the amount he was supposed to take. Withdrawal set in. He would leave home in the morning, but instead of going to work, he would drive up a canyon and sit in his car and shake. Finally, he did make it to work only to find his boss waiting for him: they could no longer keep him employed, and what was going on? Kurt just looked down at his feet and mumbled something as he walked out.

The police came at seven-thirty in the morning. With neighbors leaving for work and children standing at the bus stop, the two officers handcuffed him and hauled him off to jail. After forging prescriptions for two months, he had finally been caught.

When asked why he never let anyone know of the severity of his problem, Kurt answered that he was ashamed: ashamed of being so weak, ashamed of being unable to handle the problem on his own. He feared what his family, friends, and church leaders would think if he told them he had become addicted to prescription drugs. In retrospect, Kurt says he knows now that his silence only worsened the problem and the consequences he ultimately had to suffer.

If we are not meant to ignore, deny, or hide our weaknesses, then, what are we meant to do with them? We are to use them for our benefit. That requires us to identify and acknowledge them, face them with humility, and then, with the Lord's assistance, overcome them.

We must remember that in this process it is our direct experience with the Lord that changes us, not simply overcoming the weakness. Facing and understanding our weaknesses is merely a way of preparing us to intimately experience the Lord's benevolent care for us. That truth may be difficult to grasp, especially when self-reliance and self-control are highly valued characteristics. We know that working toward perfection includes controlling the baser instincts that accompany a mortal body, but we may mistakenly believe that is in our own ability to control, to overcome, and to subdue our weaknesses that perfection is acquired. Such efforts are important, but they are not the changing agents. Rather, it is the Lord's intervention and our experiencing his love that changes us. Control in and of itself not only is insufficient but can actually deter us from the communion with the Lord that will ultimately work the mighty change of heart.

There are at least two reasons why mere control is insufficient. First, when people with bad habits simply vow "never to do them again," after a short period of abstinence, they tend to repeat the self-defeating behavior with even greater intensity. This process is called "white knuckling it": trying to stop doing something without changing the underlying reasons that motivate the behavior in the first place. In this instance, self-control is only a way of denying that negative impulses exist. Second, if we perceive our own will and effort as being the source of positive change, more than likely we will also accept the credit for that change. In purely psychological terms, that may very well be true: bad habits can be extinguished through therapy. But that change of behavior is far from the mighty change of heart that is worked when we find our way to the source of grace—the Lord—and are touched by his benevolence. His grace transcends all psychological processes and all efforts of our own. No psychological process can replace any essential spiritual process, such as repentance. The former can be the precursor to the latter, but it will never replace it. Self-control stops us from engaging in unrighteous works. The Lord's grace frees us to do good works.

WEAKNESSES: DIVINE ORIGINS, DIVINE PURPOSES

Two important scriptures reflect the importance of acknowledging weaknesses as a way of soliciting the Lord's help in overcoming them. In Mark, we read about a father's asking Jesus to help his son. In this case, the weakness is doubt. Then "Jesus said unto him, If thou canst believe, all things are possible to him that believeth. And straightway the father of the child cried out, and said with tears, Lord, I believe; help thou mine unbelief" (Mark 9:23–24).

In this scripture, belief is paradoxically coupled with doubt in a poignant act of faith. It is not an isolated incident. Similarly, in Alma 22:18 we read: "O God, Aaron hath told me that there is a God; and if there is a God, and if thou art God, wilt thou make thyself known unto me." Again, we see the expression of faith in the very expression of doubt.

Although most of us tend to avoid facing our doubts or weaknesses because of shame or embarrassment, we need to consider the possibility that our weaknesses have divine origins that serve divine purposes. Weaknesses were given to us to foster humility. That humility helps prepare us to receive the Lord's gracious help in becoming stronger.

Weaknesses are not necessarily defects or deviations to be corrected by single exertions of priesthood power or special blessings. Neither are they to be covered up by psychological defenses that hide their true meaning and function. Weaknesses are to be faced with candor and integrity and overcome with humility and the Lord's gracious assistance.

AVOIDANCE: KEEPING WEAK THINGS WEAK

Few qualities contribute more to maintaining weaknesses than avoiding what we fear or find uncomfortable. Avoidance means denying, distorting, and rationalizing the negative things we don't care to face about ourselves or others. It is an attempt to escape from conflict and opposition because of the pain and distress they create. Avoidance compels us to distort reality as a way of making things look better than they really are.

Spiritually, we believe that conflict and opposition play an absolutely essential role in our eternal development. Avoiding those hurdles because of our fear of them limits our potential for spiritual growth. It is at these most difficult times that our weaknesses are most likely to appear. Furthermore, these moments of opposition also reveal us as we really are. Elder Neal A. Maxwell said, "Trials and tribulations tend to squeeze the artificiality out of us, leaving the essence of what we *really* are and clarifying what we *really* yearn for" (*Things as They Really Are* [Salt Lake City: Deseret Book, 1980], p. 89). If we avoid difficulty, we shun the opportunity to identify our weaknesses and overcome them. We also miss the chance to experience ourselves in our truest form—stripped of all pretense with the true desires of our heart uncovered. What a wonderful occasion to clearly evaluate ourselves and make the necessary adjustments that can bring us closer to the Lord.

The following story illustrates how deadly avoidance can be. Avoidance has many different forms and varieties, only one of which is illustrated in this example. Regardless of its forms, however, avoidance is always distinguished by an attempt to escape from unwanted or unwelcome thoughts, feelings, or events because of the fear or shame associated with them. The following story, taken from a letter, helps clarify the role of avoidance in the development of emotional problems.

"For the past several years, I have felt that my life was meaningless. This was an ironic state of affairs considering all that I had accomplished. Friends and relatives were always lauding me for my good looks and intelligence. I was the first person on either side of my family to graduate from college, doing so with honors. I had a good job with an important accounting firm. I had plenty of dates. By all outward appearances, my life was very fulfilling. Yet I was miserable and felt increasingly depressed.

"Six months of psychotherapy had helped me catch an occasional glimpse of the underlying cause of my unhappiness. It always seemed to involve low self-esteem or my disapproval of myself. Somehow, it seemed I really did have a low opinion of myself, but I found that idea confusing because of all the success in my life. Finally, I was able to put my finger on the problem. Because I had such a low opinion of myself, I believed others would think of me in the same way if they really got to know me. And then, because of that, I was unwilling to expose myself to others as the person I really was. I took great pains to sidestep high-pressure situations, to gain the approval of others, and to avoid making decisions that might reveal things about me that I didn't want others to know. I can see countless examples of this pattern in my life now that I have caught on to my style.

"My unwillingness to let myself be known probably caused me the greatest difficulty in my relationships with the women I found the most attractive. My most recent relationship is a good example. After weeks of building up courage, I finally asked her out on a date. It was quickly obvious that she liked me as much as I liked her. I should have been elated, but instead I got scared about really making myself known to this woman. I put up a fake front designed to impress her. I was petrified of becoming too vulnerable. This led to behavior that was both hot and cold as I kept testing her to see if I could let down my guard, be myself, and still be liked by her. When we broke up after eight months, I was terribly lonely. I realize now that the relationship might have had a chance to be meaningful on a long-term basis if I had had the courage to risk presenting an honest picture of myself.

"I am now amazed at how often I have chosen to avoid facing situations that would expose my true self to others—all because I don't want others to know me and dislike me the way I dislike myself."

Another deadly form of psychological avoidance is called disconfirmation. It grows out of comparing ourselves to others, and it occurs when we see and accept as true something about ourselves that we wish wasn't so. Examples could include believing we are dull, lazy, or unlikable. The particular belief doesn't matter very much, and it doesn't matter if it's true. The crucial point is that we believe it, and we wish we didn't.

The next step in the process of disconfirmation is to collect evidence to prove to ourselves that what we have already glimpsed and accepted to be true about ourselves isn't true at all. The problem with our attempts to disconfirm what we believe is that not only does it never work but it usually makes things worse. For example, if we believe we are not very bright, we may go about trying to disprove our belief by doing well in school. Grades become paramount. But no matter how well we do, someone always does better. Can improved grades eventually lead us to think of ourselves as more intelligent than we already believe we are? Not likely. We explain our success by saying "I just work harder in school than the others" and then take another, harder class to see if the first good grades were just luck.

The cycle, once started, can be endless. How much proof is enough to convince us to stop believing we aren't good enough? There is never enough! Thinking of ourselves as not very bright, for example, is a feeling of being inadequate—it's an emotion, not a fact. Just as a fear of flying is hardly ever influenced by a factual understanding of the safety performance of the airlines, so the fear of being not very bright is hardly ever influenced by good academic performance. The treadmill rolls on. We attempt to change deeply held feelings about ourselves that simply become more immune to the "proof" that we constantly strive for and yet never possess.

Jill is a typical representative of how disconfirmation works. Jill is in her twenties, attractive, sociable, and bright, yet she doubts that anybody who gets to know her would really love her. To authentically open herself up to such a relationship feels very risky. If the relationship failed, it would confirm Jill's deepest fears about her lack of attractiveness to others, particularly to men she finds attractive. So she doesn't get involved in meaningful relationships. Instead, she maximizes her superficial assets and makes herself attractive to as many men as possible. She thus appears popular and fun and is in high social demand. That provides her with constant, albeit shallow, reassurance about her attractiveness. All these relationships are orchestrated by Jill to be short-term while still providing her a daily dose of reassurance via social popularity. Nevertheless, the end of each relationship confirms Jill's deepest fears about herself: men are interested in her for only a short time and only for superficial reasons.

Essentially, then, disconfirmation is a way of trying to prove what we are not. It tells us very little about what we are. It interferes with both spiritual and psychological development because it requires us to deny feelings that frighten us. We then structure our lives to gather proof that what we already believe to be true about ourselves really is not true. But because deeply felt emotions about ourselves are seldom influenced by proof of any kind, our continuous attempts to gather evidence can go on endlessly, just as a dog chasing its own tail never catches it because the faster the dog runs, the faster its tail moves.

Careful introspection can produce insights into how this mechanism may operate in our own lives. The following exercise may increase our awareness of the most important things about ourselves we wish were not true.

SELF-EVALUATION EXERCISE

1. Are there things about yourself that you already believe to be true but deeply wish were not? For example, do you think

of yourself as unattractive, ineffective, dumb, lazy, aggressive, or uncaring? List your three most important observations.

2. Now try to increase your awareness of what you actually do or say to help you convince yourself that these things may not be true, at least not all the time. For example, do you refrain from competing in important life events as a way of refraining from finding out if you would succeed or fail, or do you keep busy as a way of covering up what you really think and feel about yourself? List your three most important insights.

3. Are those behaviors helpful to you in any important ways? Do they work? Do you approve of them? Do you want to continue them?

4. Finally, and most importantly, what would you have to do so that you could realistically and authentically approve of yourself for the way in which you handle your most handicapping fears? List your three most important observations and then discuss them openly with your most trusted friend.

HOW WEAKNESSES BECOME STRENGTHS

The first recorded incident of avoiding conflict took place as a result of Satan's influence in the Garden of Eden. The purpose of that avoidance was to deny or to hide from God something that Adam and Eve were ashamed of—a purpose that is entirely consistent with Satan's character and intent. So, if God and Satan represent opposites in character and purpose, then their preferred methods of responding to opposition and conflict are probably also opposite. If Satan advocates personal deception and dishonesty, then God must favor honesty and facing unpleasant realities just as they really are.

In scripture we read: "The Lord spake unto me, saying:

Fools mock, but they shall mourn; and my grace is sufficient for the meek, that they shall take no advantage of your weakness;

"And if men come unto me I will show unto them their weakness. I give unto men weakness that they may be humble; and my grace is sufficient for all men that humble themselves before me; for if they humble themselves before me, and have faith in me, then will I make weak things become strong unto them" (Ether 12:26–27).

What an utterly profound contrast! Whereas Satan would have us avoid facing our faults so that we may appear better than we really are, the Lord requires us to acknowledge our faults so that we may actually become better.

In psychological terms, the Lord's way of responding to opposition and conflict is called coping. Coping is acknowledging the truth about ourselves or the world in which we live instead of falsifying either to make things appear better or more pleasant than they really are. Coping is facing problems and, in so doing, attempting to make things better. It is the essence of righteous self-government.

The concept of coping has been discussed in psychological literature for decades. Generally speaking, coping is an enduring willingness to forthrightly face the very things you have a tendency to fear. It means that you are willing to face personal imperfection and that you don't have to hide from the painful things that deep down you know are true about yourself.

Coping in the Face of Conflict and Opposition

The following story illustrates the underlying motives, problems, and behaviors involved in the exercise of righteous self-government.

Colin had been deeply moved by the power of the scriptures after years of searching for the truths he had always been told they contained. His commitment to Christ had not come easily. His academic background had taught him to question, evaluate, and criticize everything he heard and read. It had proved a successful way of conducting his professional life but had not produced the sense of rightness that he sought as he pondered the words of the Lord and his prophets.

He concluded that the confirmation he sought could be experienced only if it did not come from something he was able to create on his own—logical reasoning and the satisfaction of accurately assessing the validity of something he read. As he began the fearful process of abandoning himself, a new, undeniable sensation crept into his soul. The taste of truth had never been more satisfying. Because he was a thoughtful man, it was only natural that Colin spend a lot of energy trying to determine just how someone with his spiritual understanding should live. He believed it was essential that his lifestyle be consistent with the spiritual knowledge he had acquired. Paradoxically, his desire to live more righteously quickly introduced him to a new set of real and unexpected problems.

Colin was puzzled when he first started noticing that he found participation in ward meetings spiritually unfulfilling. Gradually, it became clear why. He found fast meetings unsatisfying because of the number of dutiful parents who whispered appropriate phrases to their parroting children, members who used the time to express personal opinions rather than to share their spiritual convictions, and the congregation who seemed uninterested in what was going on and equally uninterested in doing something about it.

Similarly, he became frustrated in his elders quorum

meetings. The primary preoccupations seemed to be improving home teaching statistics, instead of service, and delving into doctrinal mysteries that could never be solved and didn't need solving in the first place. He didn't have a problem with the home teaching program or with religious speculation, but he thought his priesthood meetings should be concerned with much more than that.

He had other problems as well, but they all seemed to have one thing in common: tradition, ritual, and repetition seemed to dominate at times when he wanted the Spirit to prevail. He wanted spiritual strength—the kind he had read about so carefully in the scriptures—but he was unable to find it except when he was alone in prayerful meditation. Naturally, he was aware of the critical attitude he was developing and worried that he was the problem.

Colin found his feelings confusing and upsetting until he realized the mistake he was making. He was looking to others for the spiritual development and strength he was seeking. He was responsible for his own spiritual development; those around him were not, even those who presided over him. They could help, but it was his problem, not theirs. The help he needed had to come from his own efforts and his personal relationship with God.

Once Colin understood the problem more clearly, he began to correct it. He started by turning inward to look for the spiritual guidance he needed for his own spiritual development. As a result, he quietly and privately started helping a single parent who was really in desperate need. The family he adopted was deeply appreciative because they knew his service was motivated by something other than filling an assignment. Gradually he attained a more complete understanding of service and Christian charity. As his insights grew, so did his willingness to enhance the lives of others as the Lord had already enhanced his. Church meetings were less frustrating to him, and he became willing to serve rather than wait to be served by others.

In this story, just as in much of life, the outcome was a product of three elements. The first was the dominance of righteous intent instead of social approval and comfort. The second was the strong disposition to cope with conflict and opposition with unfeigned personal honesty and integrity instead of avoidance. The third and final element was personal responsibility. When Colin started finding his ward meetings spiritually unsatisfying, he was faced with a rather unique problem. Just who do we blame for spiritually unsatisfying meetings? Ourselves? Others? The bishopric? It is a tough question that is difficult for most of us even to think about fairly, let alone discuss openly. Ultimately, however, Colin didn't blame anyone. Instead, he asked himself and God what his spiritual needs were. But before he could ask this question, he had to face an unpleasant internal reality about himself that he probably would have preferred to avoid. That is, "What does it say about me that I find so many of my meetings spiritually unsatisfying?" Some of the potential answers to that question could have been devastating, but he asked himself anyhow. And because he was willing to cope with that internal reality in humility rather than avoid it, he was able to move on to the next step of his spiritual development.

Although Colin's is a story of a personal search for spiritual truth and understanding, it is also a story of righteous self-government. At each important decision point, what he chose to do was based on his inner spiritual promptings, which allowed him to be congruent; he became more self-directing as he abandoned his criticism of those around him; he exercised his autonomy to become self-motivated in righteous works; and he acknowledged his own failings with the intent to overcome any part of the problem of spiritual opposition that he had created himself. All of these steps are fundamental to righteous self-government. The absence of any one of them would have altered not only the outcome of Colin's story but also his path of spiritual growth.

CHAPTER NINE
....

DOING THE RIGHT THINGS
FOR THE RIGHT REASONS

DOING THE RIGHT THINGS FOR THE RIGHT REASONS grows out
of individual identity, congruence, and autonomy. Those characteristics provide the balance and support necessary to be
righteously self-governing. Without righteous self-government,
our life would be much like a ship at sea with no rudder to
guide it. We can be certain we will eventually end up somewhere, but it may not be where we intended to go. Because of
that truth, we consider these three inner forces to be the central elements of spiritual development and psychological well-
being. They interact with each other continually and are vital
in helping us achieve our life goals. We will briefly review their
essential characteristics.

Identity. Identity is our personal sense of individuality and
self-understanding that gives purpose and direction to our life.
It is our answer to the question "Who am I?" both spiritually
and psychologically. To enhance our identity requires clarifying our personal values and deeply held beliefs about the
meaning of our existence. Generally, the clearer we are about
our own values and attitudes toward life, the more likely we
are to steer our life in a direction that is both satisfying and
meaningful to us.

Congruence. Identity answers the question, "Who am I?"

129

and congruence asks, "How true am I to myself?" Congruence is the compatibility between what we appear to be on the outside and what we really are on the inside. Congruent behavior is a natural expression of our inward feelings and motives at the time we actually experience them. Because of this, congruence is synonymous with integrity. Congruence involves honesty not only with ourselves but with others as well. We are willing to openly declare and share with others our problems, concerns, motives, hopes, and wishes. Congruence is just the opposite of impression management. Enhancing congruence requires facing the risk of truly knowing ourselves and then facing the added risk of making ourselves truly known to others. Congruence is the most direct pathway from our internal/eternal identity to our outward behavior.

Autonomy. Autonomy asks of us, "What do I do with who I am?" Autonomy is inseparably linked to moral agency and the freedom to choose. Autonomy is a reflection of our capacity both to choose for ourselves freely and independently and also to immunize ourselves against the tyranny of social pressure. Enduring autonomy is a reflection of our ability to direct our life according to our own will and values in harmony with the Lord's.

JESUS, THE EPITOME OF RIGHTEOUS SELF-GOVERNMENT

The Savior was the only perfect man. According to the Prophet Joseph Smith, "None ever were perfect but Jesus; and why was He perfect? Because He was the Son of God, and had the fullness of the Spirit, and greater power than any man" (*Teachings of the Prophet Joseph Smith*, sel. Joseph Fielding Smith [Salt Lake City: Deseret Book, 1973], 187–88). The easiest way for us to strive for a similar fulness of spirit is to study and then emulate our Savior's earthly behavior. That includes his perfect ability to be righteously self-governing. His demonstration of identity, congruence, and autonomy was unflawed. His supreme knowledge of who he was required him to confirm his identity even to those who would condemn and kill him. His honesty manifested itself in a constant congruence of thought, feeling, and behavior, even when corrupt priests and Pharisees tried to ensnare him with their deceptive questions and accusations. Even when his closest disciple denied him and his Father in Heaven left him to suffer alone, the Savior chose, with full autonomy, to accept his godly calling. Perfect righteousness could demand no less.

CONCLUSION

The essence of righteous self-government is Christlike behavior born of Christlike thoughts and feelings. In the process of achieving this spiritual ideal, righteous self-government demands congruence between what we truly are and what we present ourselves to be. It asks us to strip away pretense and acknowledge the reality of our nature, whether good or bad, acceptable or unacceptable. We must be willing to pluck out the beam in our own eye. Our ability to do that is enhanced by the precision and clarity with which we comprehend our own unique internal/eternal identity, exercise our capacity to act congruently with the dictates of that identity in good times and bad, and cultivate our ability to freely and autonomously make decisions based on righteous intent, particularly in the face of conflict and opposition. Then, and only then, in facing what we are, can we become what we can be.

There is spiritual and psychological power in doing the

right things for the right reasons. By combining good works with worthy intent, we maintain personal integrity, which allows us to be open with the Lord, ourselves, and others. And is there anything more compelling than the individual who has nothing to hide and speaks without deception or guile? Integrity makes us more sensitive to our weaknesses and sins, but it also gives us the desire and strength to overcome them.

Exercising our identities with congruence and autonomy can leave us vulnerable to the rejection and ridicule of those who place social acceptance above the acceptance of the Savior. But when the clamoring of such individuals fades away, we will be left with an enduring sense of peace if we remain true to our internal/eternal selves.

We suggest that doing the right things for the right reasons is evidenced in the following situations to the degree they reflect who and what we really are:

When we look around and see the poverty and pain among God's children, and because we have seen the needless reality of so much suffering we actually hurt for others, and because we hurt for others we work to help them only because we care.

When we stand trembling over a spouse or child in the administration of the priesthood waiting endlessly to speak until the Spirit gives utterance rather than offering appropriate and traditional words.

When we stand over the coffin of a loved one and at the moment of our greatest grief, simultaneously feel the spiritual assurance that mortality is but a small moment of eternity.

When we have a lesson or talk to give in Church and really collaborate with the Lord in our preparation rather than just being competently prepared to fill our assignment.

When we kneel in family prayer each night, not out of

habit, duty, or obligation but out of love and gratitude for the blessings in our family and the craving for God's spirit to grace our home.

When we bring a truly broken heart and a contrite spirit to our partaking of the sacrament on Sunday so that accepting the emblems of the body and blood of Christ is a spiritual event rather than just a ritual.

When we believe deep within ourselves that we are in need of greater humility, and with fear and trembling ask the Lord to teach us humility realizing that we are also in need of courage to face the lessons we may be about to face.

Even though these events are the kind that bring us closer to God, they seldom bring us the admiration of others. They are more powerful and enduring, but they are also more modest, internal, and are rarely known by others. It is in these moments of spiritual privacy, where real and humble intent prevails over pleasing appearances, that righteous self-government is acquired.

As we strive to do the right things for the right reasons, we can look to such great men as Nephi, who never faltered in the face of persecution by his own family; to Captain Moroni, who refused to accept the social evils of his time; to Joseph Smith, who faced martyrdom rather than deny what he knew was true; and to the Savior, who in all moments of his life, regardless of situation or consequence, was *real*—real in the sense that what he was on earth was the same as he would be throughout eternity: pure in thought, feeling, and behavior. He is the epitome of righteous self-government, the Exemplar, providing an example that can lead us to peace if we are willing to be honest with ourselves and with him.

INDEX

Actions, 80–82, 96
Adam and Eve, 29, 77, 114, 123
Agency, 77–78, 83–85, 130
Appearances: society values
    outward, 2; example of
    wealthy woman, 7–9
Approval: need for, 11, 26; as
    motivator, 19; story of woman
    dependent upon, 45–46
Auschwitz, Nazi death camp at, 34
Autonomy: component of
    righteous self-government, 19;
    Savior's example of, 22;
    definition of, 75, 95–96;
    personal, exercise, 75–76;
    spiritual, 76–80; components
    of, 77; psychological, 80–85;
    not spiritually dangerous,
    83–84; stifled by shame, 86–90;
    epitomized by charity, 91–95;
    review of, 130
Avoidance, 118–20, 123–24

Baseball hitter slump, example of,
    42
Beams, 97–98, 108; types of
    psychological, 98–99
Behaving intentionally, 71
Behavior, Christlike, 131
Bishop's interview with young
    couple, example of, 78–80
Black-and-white thinkers, 45
Bradshaw, John, 87

Calvin, example of, 53–55
Change: self scrutiny fuels, 3;

personal process of, 5; comes
    from Lord, 116–17
Change of heart, 3, 15, 51–52,
    116–17
Charity: Paul's sermon on, 16, 52;
    definition of, 53; stories of
    young men striving to gain,
    53–55, 91–95
Childhood: incongruity stems
    from, 67; beliefs influence
    adulthood, 100; life scripts
    received during, 106–8
Choice, 32, 80–82, 85, 130
Christ, as source of change,
    116–17
Christlike behavior, 131
Christmas letter, example of,
    10–11
Church: callings in, and motives
    in fulfilling, 17–19; story of
    young man who finds
    meetings in, unfilling, 125–27
Cindy, example of, 45–46
Clint, example of, 69
Colin, example of, 125–27
College, story of young man
    deciding to attend, 84–85
Conflict, 118
Conformity, mindless, 27–28
Congruence: liberating power of,
    5; component of righteous
    self-government, 19; Savior's
    example of, 21–22; lack of, is
    harmful, 35; definition of, 57,
    59; personal, exercise, 57–59;

135

Repentance, 3, 51–52, 56, 117
Responsibility, personal, 126–27
Righteous self-government:
definition of, 3–4, 15, 51; goal
of, 5; steps of, 14, 127–28; more
than good behavior, 16;
components of, 19–22; power of,
131–32; examples of, 132–33
Righteousness, as result of
overcoming weaknesses, 113
Risk, 88–89, 130
Rogers, Carl, 61
Role models, 133

Satan, 123–24
Savior: knowing the, 48; overall
example of, 130–31, 133; as
example of righteous self-
government, 19–22; as
example of identity, 19–21; as
example of congruence, 21–22;
as example of autonomy, 22
Screwtape Letters, 97
Secrets, danger of, 89
Self-approval strengthens identity,
43
Self-control is insufficient, 116–17
Self-criticism, 101
Self-directing, being, 75
Self-discovery is a goal of
mortality, 29
Self-evaluation, 59–61; Nephi's
example of, 60–61; value of, 66
Self-image, story of man with
poor, 119–20
Self-restraint, 15
Service, 34, 91–95; motives
behind, 17–19
Shame: stifles autonomy, 86;
healthy or toxic, 87, 89–90;
suggestions for overcoming,
87–90; power of, 90
Sharon, example of, 64–67
Sick friend, example of visiting,
62–63
Sister Jackson, example of, 101–3
Smith, Joseph, 31, 47–48, 130
Social conditioning, 9–11
Society's influence, 2, 55
Solution oriented, becoming, 42–44

Spirit: discerning the, 79–80;
direction from the, 96
Spirits, eternal nature of, 31–32
Spiritual self, knowing our, 48
Stella, example of, 23–26
Steve, example of, 84–85
Stool, three-legged, 19
Strength, psychological, 90–91
Suicide, study of attempts at,
among university students, 33

Talmage, James E., 20, 51
Test, mortality is a, 113
Testimony, 47
Testimony meeting, 11
Three-legged stool, 19
Tim, example of, 59–60
Toxic shame, 87, 89–90
Trials, 118
True believer, the, 22, 26–28
Truth: eternal, 61–62; facing the,
66, 68–69

Unattractive, example of young
woman who fears she is, 121–22
Urim and Thummim, 5

Victims of circumstance, 81
Visiting Teaching, 63

Walter, John, 43
Weaknesses: hiding our, 3, 111,
113–16; acknowledging and
facing, 4, 72, 113; Lord will help
us overcome, 55, 124; how to
use, for our benefit, 116; divine
purposes of, 117–18; become
strengths, 123–28
Wealth, worldly, 11–12
Wealthy New Hampshire woman,
example of, 7–9
"White knuckling it," 116
Willpower, 15
Win-lose, 91
Win-win, 91
Works, good, 16
Worldly things bring no
satisfaction, 9

Yalom, Irvin, 33